WELCOME

His name resonates down through the decades and stands alongside such illustrious men as George Washington, Abraham Lincoln, and Franklin D Roosevelt. In their own individual ways, each changed the course of history and so it was with JFK, who dared to strive for the abolition of racial discrimination, to face down ideological enemies and to challenge humans to land on the Moon, to "ask what you can do for your country" and reinvigorate in a new generation the call for service and duty – not in war but in times of peace.

More than that, however, in examining the life and times of John Fitzgerald Kennedy we pick apart the nuances of a different age, a time of unprecedented change when the world shared a vibrant new wave of popular music with warnings about imminent nuclear war and challenges to international peace. A time shared with grand ambitions for a new decade of technical change and human progress, for a desire to engage with a life of promise and prosperity unfettered from poverty and ignorance.

On the 60th anniversary of his assassination, we look back at a life born to privilege but spent campaigning for the rights of every man and woman to enjoy a safe and secure life and to fulfil their potential. Yet for all that, it is the story of a life carrying the burden of human flaws, at times blighted by indiscretion. In that regard this is not the story of a flawless leader, rather the collective experiences of flawed humans, and as such it is hoped to present a realistic portrayal of political power, privilege, and personal ambition.

Over the next several chapters we track the tense drama of a sometimes mercurial life and collisions with seismic events which include a decision to send Americans to the Moon, the struggle to maintain freedom for the citizens of a divided Berlin, to stem the fanatical onward rush of an unconstrained and home-grown arms race and to face down a direct challenge to the Western world and a nuclear war over missiles on Cuba.

To help understand the part played by aides and advisers, there is a potted biography of key players and the roles they played in the Kennedy Presidency of 1961-1963. Along the way we follow the ever-changing vicissitudes of the Kennedy family, their legacy now enshrined by three members of that dynasty serving the United States in various government roles.

Politics played a central role in the Kennedy family, but this is not an exclusively political story, it is also about ambition and about feuds, within and outside the family itself. Few since Kennedy have achieved such universal acclaim, nor received such controversial judgement on their lives and their presidency. History will judge if either view is correct, or whether there is a blended cocktail of each, in the remarkable and distinguished life of John Fitzgerald Kennedy which we unpick over the following pages.

David Baker
Author

> "This is not an exclusively political story, it is also about ambition and about feuds, within and outside the family itself."

BELOW: JFK delivers a speech at Rice University in 1962 where he declares that America is going to the Moon "not because it is easy, but because it is hard," as a motivation for a national revival in science and technology (NASA)

CONTENTS

06 WINNING DAYS
The early life of the Kennedy family, their political ambitions, and the presidential election of 1960.

14 FIRST LADY
The life and times of Jackie Kennedy and the trials and tribulations of a President's wife in the 1960s.

20 THE BELTWAY BOYS
A new breed of politician brings change to the political scene in Washington as social norms are ignored.

26 THE FAMOUS FIXERS
A dive into the lives and personalities of aids, assistants, and key players in the Kennedy years.

32 TO THE MOON!
Kennedy responds to Soviet space 'firsts' with a commitment to send astronauts to the lunar surface by the end of the decade.

46 THE ARMS RACE
JFK wrestles with rumours of a missile gap with the Russians while challenging calls for more US weapons.

56 BERLIN
As Russian troops back East German forces to expel Allied forces from Berlin, Kennedy faces down a military threat.

96

06

CONTENTS

70 THE CUBAN MISSILE CRISIS
Khrushchev puts Soviet rockets on the island of Cuba and brings the world to the brink of war.

88 CULTURE WARS
Changes to the social scene in the 1960s as a revolution brings new music and a wave of protest movements.

92 FEUDING FAMILIES
The Kennedy and Johnson families disagree and competition fuels discord and animosity as tensions rise.

96 THE ASSASSINATION
The President visits Dallas and an assassin with a troubled background fires the fatal shots.

104 LEGACY
How decisions made by Kennedy set in motion events which would live on for several decades and influence future generations.

112 CHRONOLOGY – A LIFE IN TIME
A timeline of the key periods in the life of JFK and the events surrounding his Presidency.

46

56

20

ISBN: 978 1 80282 810 8
Editor: David Baker
Senior editor, specials: Roger Mortimer
Email: roger.mortimer@keypublishing.com
Cover design: Steve Donovan
Design: SJmagic DESIGN SERVICES, India
Advertising Sales Manager: Brodie Baxter
Email: brodie.baxter@keypublishing.com
Tel: 01780 755131
Advertising Production: Becky Antoniades
Email: Rebecca.antoniades@keypublishing.com

SUBSCRIPTION/MAIL ORDER
Key Publishing Ltd, PO Box 300, Stamford, Lincs, PE9 1NA
Tel: 01780 480404
Subscriptions email: subs@keypublishing.com

Mail Order email: orders@keypublishing.com
Website: www.keypublishing.com/shop

PUBLISHING
Group CEO: Adrian Cox
Publisher, Books and Bookazines: Jonathan Jackson
Published by
Key Publishing Ltd, PO Box 100, Stamford, Lincs, PE9 1XQ
Tel: 01780 755131 **Website:** www.keypublishing.com

PRINTING
Precision Colour Printing Ltd, Haldane, Halesfield 1, Telford, Shropshire. TF7 4QQ

DISTRIBUTION
Seymour Distribution Ltd, 2 Poultry Avenue, London, EC1A 9PU
Enquiries Line: 02074 294000.

We are unable to guarantee the bona fides of any of our advertisers. Readers are strongly recommended to take their own precautions before parting with any information or item of value, including, but not limited to money, manuscripts, photographs, or personal information in response to any advertisements within this publication.

© Key Publishing Ltd 2023
All rights reserved. No part of this magazine may be reproduced or transmitted in any form by any means, electronic or mechanical, including photocopying, recording or by any information storage and retrieval system, without prior permission in writing from the copyright owner. Multiple copying of the contents of the magazine without prior written approval is not permitted.

CHAPTER ONE

WINNING DAYS

John Fitzgerald Kennedy, the second son to Joseph Patrick Kennedy Snr and Rose Elizabeth Kennedy (nee Fitzgerald), was born in Brookline, Massachusetts on May 29, 1917, to a world in convulsions and dramatic change. Events would see life transformed by social upheaval, technological inventions, unprecedented economic growth, a major financial collapse, and dynamic political change sweeping away kings and nations. New forms of autocratic rule would consume democracies in Russia, Italy, and Germany and America would bask in its newfound position as the world's richest country.

The United States had just entered the conflict in Europe which had been raging since August 1914, in Britain the royal family was about to change its German name to Windsor, and in France 30,000 troops had just mutinied. But in Brookline there was little attention to those events as the Kennedy family celebrated the birth of a son, their attentions far from issues of international affairs and the vicissitudes of political life.

Joseph Kennedy himself had experienced some of that turbulence. Born on September 6, 1888 in Boston, Massachusetts, he was the elder son of Mary Augusta Kennedy and the politician Patrick Joseph Kennedy, a family of Irish immigrants from New Ross, County Wexford, fleeing the potato famine.

ABOVE: The official portrait of John Fitzgerald Kennedy, 35th President of the United States from the inauguration on January 20, 1961 to his assassination on November 22, 1963. (White House)

ABOVE: Joseph P Kennedy Snr (1888-1969) fathered nine children between 1915 and 1932 and created a dynasty with politically active members of Congress and local government. (NARA)

Joseph excelled in sports and graduated from Boston Latin School in 1908 and then from Harvard with a degree in economics, marrying Rose in October 1914 before settling in to their home in a suburb of Boston before the birth of the first son, Joseph P Kennedy Jnr on July 26, 1915.

Joseph Snr had a skill in making money and amassed a small fortune from commodity investment and as a stock broker, moving his money into film studios, property, and shipping. His sense of timing was the secret to his fortune, built up quickly and through a wide range of contacts. Some of these, including Frank Costello of the Italian Luciano crime family, would claim later that he had been involved in some of their dealings but there has never been any conclusive evidence to prove that.

Later, in the Great Depression of 1929 he redirected his fortune into property deals and increased his wealth from $4m to $180m six years later, approximately $4bn today. Prioritising the financial security of his family, Joseph used his money to set up lifelong trust funds for his children which ensured them financial independence for the rest of their lives. In all, Joseph and Rose had nine children. After Joseph Jnr and JFK, came Rosemary in 1918, Kathleen Agnes in 1920, Eunice Mary in 1921, Patricia in 1924, Robert in 1925, Jean in 1928, and Edward in 1932.

A strong supporter of Roosevelt in his successful bid for the presidency, in 1934 Joseph Kennedy became the first chairman of the Securities and Exchange Commission (SEC), set up that year to constrain

ABOVE: JFK in football gear at Dexter School, Massachusetts in 1926. (JFK Presidential Library)

That appointment shocked many who regarded Kennedy's philandering ways and womanising as inappropriate, and rumours of dealings with unsavoury characters and Mafia bosses, while never proven, stuck. It was during his tenure as ambassador that Joseph Kennedy lost a lot of the shine from his reputation for straight-talking and productive decision-making. His strident pro-Irish, outspoken disapproval of the British lost him support on both sides of the Atlantic Ocean.

In believing that fascism was the way of the future he criticised Winston Churchill's stand against Hitler, siding with Chamberlain and supporting a negotiated deal with Germany. With exalted hubris, he embarrassed the Roosevelt administration and was condemned first by the US political elite and then by the British themselves who came to see him as a representative of anti-British, isolationist policies.

When war broke out in September 1939, Joseph Snr had declared: "Democracy is finished in England…the whole reason for aiding England is to give us time…As long as she is there, we have time to prepare…I know more about the European situation than anybody else." In a somewhat prescient appraisal of his ambitions, the British MP Josiah Wedgewood IV wrote that: "We have a rich man, untrained in diplomacy, unlearned in history and politics, who is a great publicity seeker and who is apparently ambitious to be the first Catholic President."

Concerned at his extremist views, Roosevelt had him recalled to make a radio speech endorsing the government's line on helping free democracies with uncommitted aid. That, to secure the Catholic vote in America ahead of the presidential election on November 5,

speculation on money markets and put a stop to the market manipulation responsible for the Wall St crash of 1929. Thus, launched on a political career, Joseph Snr was appointed chairman of the US Maritime Commission in 1934 and from 1938 was Roosevelt's ambassador to Britain until 1940.

> "The United States had just entered the conflict in Europe which had been raging since August 1914, in Britain the royal family was about to change its German name to Windsor, and in France 30,000 troops had just mutinied."

ABOVE: The Kennedy family home at Brookline, Massachusetts and the place where JFK was born, now frequented by tourists around the year and from across the world. (Library of Congress)

www.keymilitary.com 7

CHAPTER ONE

1940. It also troubled Roosevelt that in Britain, MI5 had evidence implicating one of Ambassador Kennedy's aides, Tyler Kent, in cooperating with the Soviet Union and pretending to be a pro-Nazi spy to obtain and convey intelligence information from the US Embassy to the Kremlin about American communications with Berlin.

Throughout, Rose Kennedy maintained a strong family home, moving from Brookline to a house at Hyannis Port on Cape Cod. While supporting her husband she reluctantly tolerated his indiscretions which included an affair with Gloria Swanson, a famed American actress. For some time prior to the birth of Kathleen in February 1920 she stayed at her parents' home only to learn on her return that divorce would never be possible and that their marriage was insoluble.

Pressures on their public and private lives took its toll on Rose, who used prescription drugs to relieve the stress and personal nervousness brought about by the skewed marriage. A committed Catholic, she maintained a stoic silence for much of her life, constraining the troubles she endured. But her devout sense of duty as a mother was unshaken and perhaps an antidote to those pressures: "I looked on child rearing not only as a work of love and a duty, but as a profession that was fully as interesting and challenging as any honourable profession in the world and one that demanded the best I could bring to it…What greater aspiration and challenge are there for a mother than the hope of raising a great son or daughter?"

LIVED TO THE FULL

Jack Kennedy was a sickly boy who contracted more than the usual set of ailments and childhood illnesses. With a face full of smiles and with deep blue eyes, he was small for his age and on his medical card were noted that he had whooping cough, measles, chicken pox and, still yet to reach his third birthday, scarlet fever. This was a life-threatening disease at the time, highly contagious and of deep concern to his father who, for all his indiscretions, was a devoted parent.

Jack's persistent health issues brought dark humour, the family joking that it was more than a mosquito's life was worth to bite him! The family moved houses a few blocks away from their original dwelling in Brookline when Jack was three, a delightful home with turreted windows, 12 rooms, a large porch, and trimmed gardens. A complex and contradictory man, Jack's father was never happier than when providing for his family, supporting their material needs and together with Rose,

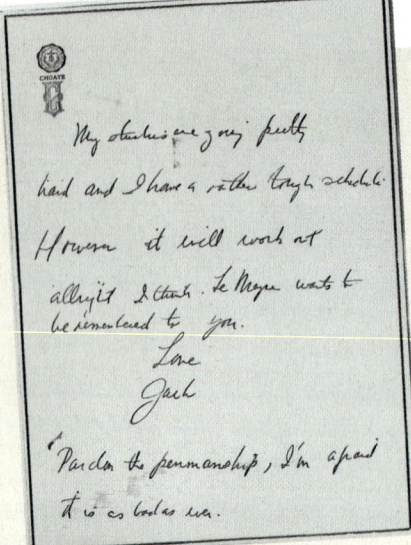

ABOVE: A letter from JFK when he was at Choate School in 1935 complaining about the intensity of the curriculum and apologising for his poor handwriting. (NARA)

> "Jack's persistent health issues brought dark humour, the family joking that it was more than a mosquito's life was worth to bite him!"

creating a peaceful environment for what was a rapidly expanding household.

By the time Jack was eight he had six siblings and there were always nannies and housekeepers to keep things in order under the loving attentions of their mother. School was chosen to give Jack exposure to a Protestant environment where Catholics had a hard time in the Boston area, his father insisting that if he were to get on in the world, he would benefit from that.

Vacations at the family summer home in Hyannis Port, Cape Cod, would bring opportunity for swimming, touch football, sailing and generally messing about in a life lived to the full. But not without its cost. When challenged to a cycle race with his elder brother Joe, Jack collided head-on, incurring superficial injuries requiring 28 stitches. With Joe being two years older than Jack, it frequently ended up that way! But as the eldest, Joe had a self-assurance fuelled by his father's professed intention that his first son would rise to great heights on the political ladder with open expectations that he would reach the White House.

Competition was revived when Jack joined Joe at the preparatory Choate boarding school in Wallingford, Connecticut. Joe had already been there for two years. Joe was seriously intent on fulfilling his father's expectations and pitched into serious learning. Seemingly forever in the shadow of his older brother, Jack resorted to mischievous pranks, gathering a supporting cast of junior 'rogues' intent on disruptive tricks including an exploding toilet seat equipped with a powerful firework!

For these and other offences to good order and discipline the 'rogues' were nearly expelled but the threat was rescinded, and some degree of normality resumed, largely due to the efforts of influential fathers and tolerant staff. But Jack was never the student his father hoped he would be and resignation to his second son's frivolous approach to study can be found in a letter he wrote while Jack was still at Choate: "I am not expecting too much, and I will not be disappointed if you don't turn out to be

ABOVE: Typical of the patrol boat class that Jack Kennedy commanded during operations in the Pacific Ocean where he was decorated for bravery rescuing sailors from the sea. (US Navy)

ABOVE: Kennedy served with the Navy in a variety of assignments, here seen on the patrol boat PT-109 in which he would receive further damage to his back injury from football. (NARA)

his father and when war broke out on September 1, 1939, he drafted a thesis on why Britain was unprepared for war, later published as a book under the title *Why England Slept*. Jack graduated from Harvard in June 1940 just as Britain was beginning its greatest struggle for survival in modern times. Both Joe and Jack joined the US Navy, a decision which would be fateful for the eldest son.

Jack had wanted to join the army but his chronically bad back prevented that and he was held on reserve under a 4-F classification due to his spinal injury, his ulcers, and other persistent ailments. Until October 1941 that is, when his father got a sympathetic Boston doctor to give Jack a satisfactory bill of health and Captain Allan Goodrich Kirk approved him for service, drafting him to a desk job at the Office of Naval Intelligence. To his father it was unthinkable that Jack would sit out the war as an invalid.

While there he came close to being cashiered over an illicit affair with Danish-born Inga Arvad, a women who had previously had many friends in the Nazi hierarchy and been introduced to Hitler before settling in the US. As a resident alien, Inga was on the FBI 'watch list' and was married to Paul Fejos. It was while under surveillance that her dalliance with Jack Kennedy came to light. Because of

a real genius, but I think you can be a really worthwhile citizen with good judgment and understanding."

Jack was happiest reading history and studying English, which he adored, following Joe to Harvard in 1936 where he began to excel at football and showed a gritty determination largely brought about by his own determination not to simply accept an implied 'second best' in both physical sports and academic achievement. Jack was mildly irritated by Joe's persistent claim that he would become President of the Unites States. But one day Jack's enthusiasm for performance on the football field gave him a lifelong back injury when he ruptured a disc in his spine.

When his father had been appointed ambassador to Britain, Jack went along and was fascinated by the tide of events across Europe where the fascists ran Italy, the Nazis governed in Germany, communist Russia was commanding a Soviet Union and Spain was importing its own unique brand of fascism under General Franco. Merging these experiences with his love of history and the English language, Jack pitched fully into a study of what to him were absorbing and rapidly evolving tides of political change.

Jack spent much time travelling the cities of Europe, the Soviet Union, the Balkans, the Middle East, and Berlin, where he was given a secret message by a US diplomat to take back to his father in London proclaiming the imminent outbreak of war. Jack was also sent as his father's representative to organise survivors from the *SS Athenia* which had been sunk by Germany west of Ireland on September 3, 1939 with the loss of 117 passengers and crew including 28 Americans.

Back at Harvard Jack pursued these studies and remained in close contact with

ABOVE: The last photograph of Joseph P Kennedy Jnr taken on August 12, 1944 before he was killed in a flying accident after taking off from East Anglia, England on a dangerous mission. (NARA)

CHAPTER ONE

ABOVE: Running for the Presidential election in 1960, JFK used television to outperform Republican nominee Richard Nixon and gain additional voter support. (White House)

that he was moved to South Carolina in January 1942.

On September 17 he completed a Naval Reserve Officer training programme and immediately volunteered for the Motor Torpedo Boat Training Center in Melville, Rhode Island where he was promoted to lieutenant. He graduated with high marks on December 2 and was asked to remain there as an instructor, but he balked at that and was assigned to Motor Torpedo Squadron 4 (MTS-4) to command PT-101, a Hughes PT boat with a length of 24m (78ft). Cheap to build and fast, they had manoeuvrability and were considered effective against many surface vessels where they could approach at high speed, let loose torpedoes fired from the decks and escape.

Jack had taken every opportunity to get aboard boats during boyhood vacations, learning from Joe how to handle sails, navigate and generally keep a deck trimmed and shipshape. Jack had collected scrimshaw, whales' teeth etched and coloured with sailing ship designs. He was a natural sailor and found new energy and an intensely competitive urge to win at all costs, challenging other PT boats to reckless races which did little to impress superiors. Fellow naval comrades found in him a decidedly different man, almost ruthless in his determination to outdo the competition.

Assigned to command of PT-109 based on Tulagi Island in the Solomons, on the night of August 1-2, 1943 along with 14 other PT boats Jack was sent out to stop four Japanese destroyers and their floatplanes carrying soldiers, sailors, and food to Kolombangara Island. In total, 24 torpedoes were launched against these ships, but none struck their targets.

But Jack caught sight of a Japanese destroyer heading north out of the island and turned to intercept it when PT-109 was struck by the destroyer *Amagiri*, slicing it in two and killing two crew members. In spite of injuries and wracked with pain, Jack towed a badly burned sailor to safety, the man's lifebelt cord strapped between his teeth.

> "When challenged to a cycle race with his elder brother Joe, Jack collided head-on, incurring superficial injuries requiring 28 stitches."

Jack's days in the navy continued with command of PT-59, rescuing 40-50 Marines from an action off Choiseul Island but his increasingly troublesome back and recent injuries saw him relieved of command and sent to a hospital on Tulagi. As his condition deteriorated, Jack's wartime service ended via extended medical treatment at Chelsea Naval Hospital on the East Coast from May to December 1944 and an honourable discharge in March, 1945.

A NEW LIFE

By this time, the Kennedy family were mourning the loss of Joe, who had been killed over the English Channel on August 12, 1944 flying a daring mission against possible V2 rocket sites on Mimoyecques, France. Code named Operation Aphrodite, it involved a converted US Navy PB4Y-1 Liberator packed with 9,600kg (21,170lb) of high explosive. After taking off from RAF Fersfield in Norfolk the two crew members, Joe Kennedy and his co-pilot John Willy were to have configured the bomber for remote control from two accompanying Lockheed Venturas but shortly after arming the explosives and before they could bale out as planned, the aircraft exploded, wreckage falling near RAF Manston.

Long before Jack got home to Massachusetts, his father had already decided to put all his cards on his second son for high political office and before the war was over, he had begun to consolidate the Kennedy name further by a ship launch ceremony, naming a warship the USS *Joseph P Kennedy Jr* in memory of his late son. The mantle had passed to the second son, who took upon himself the expectations of the family. Jack abandoned plans to become a teacher and a writer for the cut-and-thrust life of a politician.

There was never any doubt, either in his own mind or that of the family that Jack would run for Congress as a Democrat at the election. His father successfully persuaded Representative James Michael Curley to vacate the 11th District of Massachusetts seat for a position as mayor of Boston so that his son could stand for election in his stead. With almost limitless Kennedy money, Jack stood on the unimaginative slogan of "The New Generation Offers a Leader" advocating improved housing, better support for war veterans and better social conditions. Against the national trend where the Republicans took control of the House of Representatives, "JFK on the ticket OK?" got a 73% majority when the votes were counted on November 5, 1946.

Jack would serve in the House of Representatives for the next six years and focused on education and labour issues together with working hard for veteran organisations trying to alleviate some of the distress caused by the large number of servicemen finding themselves queuing for jobs. The massive cuts in government spending introduced by President Truman when he became President on the death of Franklin Roosevelt in April 1945 shifted many voters from Democratic to Republican nominees.

With his extensive knowledge of foreign affairs and his experience in Europe during

> "On September 1, 1939, he drafted a thesis on why Britain was unprepared for war, later published as a book."

1938 Jack supported the Truman Doctrine which promised US support for democracies threatened by totalitarian or communist regimes. With some reservations he also supported the 'lost China' concerns over the rapid communist takeover of that country and the almost complete absence of an appropriate American response. Jack also supported the proposal to help Italy fend off communist elements by allocating US government funds helping shore up the fragile democracy.

After three terms as a member of the House of Representatives, JFK made the next step to enter the US Senate and began preparations for that as early as 1949. The first opportunity came with the 1952 election where he ran against Henry Cabot Lodge Jnr, ably assisted by his younger brother Robert the campaign manager. Once again, his father produced the funds and the rest of the family pitched in to ease Jack up on to the next rung on the ladder. It worked and he got the Massachusetts seat by 51% to 48% when the votes were cast on November 4.

Historians would claim this as one of the most significant dates in the political history of the United States because it marked the end of the Cabot Lodge dynasty and beginning of another one – that of the Kennedys which would see Jack get all the way to the White House. But it was a tough challenge as Jack fought illness and medical treatment. All the while he had been courting Jacqueline Bouvier and they married on June 25, 1953. Her story is told in the next chapter.

Combining his duties as senator with those of his constituents, Jack led a busy life, constrained largely because of his medical condition. Several times he was not expected to live and on more than one occasion was awarded the last rites by his Catholic priest. All the time, nursing a love of writing, he produced a book, *Profiles in Courage* about powerful political figures who struggled against adversity and criticism but remained true to their convictions and achieved great things. It won the Pulitzer Prize for 1957, but Ted Sorenson would claim that he had written a lot of it for Jack.

On November 4, 1958 JFK was returned for a second session as senator for Massachusetts, this time winning by 73% to 26% against his opponent, Vincent Celeste. JFK's performance over the preceding six

years had endeared him to the electorate, his attendance to their concerns lauded and the time spent supporting state issues bringing its own reward at the ballot box. The upward profile was not a foregone conclusion, although the family reputation helped bring success and the family money ensured ample publicity whenever that was required.

JFK's formal bid for the presidency was announced on January 2, 1960, for the nomination of the Democratic Party and the election on November 8. Again, Robert would be Jack's campaign manager with Larry O'Brien and Kenneth O'Donnell key players in welding the team together as well as securing the Irish vote. The campaign got a strong start and Kennedy was keen to enter as many primaries as possible to increase his chances. He saw Hubert Humphrey off at the Wisconsin primary, but they contested against each other at the West Virginia primary. Despite being away from his strong Catholic base, JFK held the first of those but failed to knock Humphrey completely out of the running.

Nevertheless, when he entered the convention, he brought the most delegates and the sheer professionalism of the campaign secured that for him at the first ballot. It was a more difficult decision choosing a running mate for vice president and while Robert wanted the union leader and civil rights campaigner Walther Reuther, Jack went for Lyndon Johnson to ensure stronger support from the southern states. When he won the Democratic Party nomination on July 13, 1960, JFK began his New Frontiers campaign in earnest, calling forth all the issues that would remain his priorities in office.

ABOVE: A portrait of JFK during the 1952 Congressional election where he beat Henry Cabot Lodge to a seat in the Senate. (NARA)

ABOVE: JFK casts a vote for himself at the Boston Public Library during the 1960 Presidential election which he won by a very narrow margin. (NARA)

CHAPTER ONE

BELOW: The inauguration ceremony on January 20, 1961 where JFK is sworn in along with the Vice President, Lyndon Johnson. (JFK Library)

Running against Republican candidate and vice president Richard Nixon, a crucial part of the campaign was four televised debates each lasting one hour, and which would mark a new era in US elections. The first was held on September 26, 1960 and after opening statements each candidate got 2min 30sec to answer questions put by the moderator. Nixon was visibly sweating, on edge and clamouring to hold up. Mayor Daley was shocked by his faltering appearance and commented "My God, they've embalmed him before he even died!"

The second debate on October 7 had no opening remarks or closing statements and Nixon did a little better. As he did on the third appearance on October 13 when military matters were discussed, Nixon having to repeat the Eisenhower policy while JFK could range far and wide across options. The fourth and last TV debate was held on October 21 and general foreign affairs were discussed.

Public reaction to the debates was mixed but Nixon was clearly not a polished speaker. Where JFK exuded confidence and appeared certain of his opinions, Nixon seemed less sure and in difficulty as he tried to separate himself sufficiently from the Eisenhower policies and find a new range of alternatives to critical judgement over the incumbent's track record.

It all came down to the polling booth and on November 8, 1960 it went right down to the wire, with Kennedy getting 49.7% of the popular vote to Nixon's 49.5%. It was the narrowest of wins, a mere 113,000 votes between them: about the population of a small mid-Western town. Because of

ABOVE: The inaugural parade watched by several thousand spectators in a lavish and orchestrated ceremony culminating in an evening celebratory ball. (NARA)

12 JFK – A LIFE REMEMBERED

the different sizes of the electoral districts, Kennedy carried 22 States to Nixon's 26. It was historic because, with Alaska and Hawaii admitted to the Union this was the first time 50 States were involved. But the Electoral College voted Kennedy 303 against 219 for Nixon and that was decisive.

When John Fitzgerald Kennedy was sworn in as the 35th President of the United States on a very cold, clear winter morning in front of the Capitol on January 20, 1961, the world watched as the youngest man to achieve that office swore an oath to serve the nation. His tone was self-assured, firm and he had a clear message of hope and anticipation. Nobody could know that in the first year alone he would face unexpected challenges, threats, and crises. But his declaration of intent was clear:

"We observe today not a victory of party but a celebration of freedom - symbolizing an end as well as a beginning - signifying renewal as well as change. For I have sworn before you and Almighty God the same solemn oath our forebears prescribed nearly a century and three-quarters ago.

"The world is very different now. For man holds in his mortal hands the power to abolish all forms of human poverty and all forms of human life. And yet the same revolutionary beliefs for which our forebears fought are still at issue around the globe - the belief that the rights of man come not from the generosity of the state but from the hand of God.

"We dare not forget today that we are the heirs of that first revolution. Let the word go forth from this time and place, to friend and foe alike, that the torch has been passed to a new generation of Americans – born in this century, tempered by war, disciplined by a hard and bitter peace, proud of our ancient heritage – and unwilling to witness or permit the slow undoing of those human rights to which this nation has always been committed, and to which we are committed today at home and around the world.

"Let every nation know, whether it wishes us well or ill, that we shall pay any price, bear any burden, meet any hardship, support any friend, oppose any foe to assure the survival and the success of liberty."

ABOVE: Members of the Kennedy administration's cabinet are sworn in on January 21, 1961. (NARA)

ABOVE: President Kennedy visited Ireland in late June 1963 and is seen here in a motorcade through the streets of Dublin to rapturous acclaim. (NARA)

CHAPTER TWO

THE FIRST LADY

The story of John Fitzgerald Kennedy would be incomplete without that of his wife, Jacqueline Kennedy, born Jacqueline Lee Bouvier on July 28, 1929 in the Southampton Hospital, New York. As the wife of the President, Jackie inherited media attention and worldwide recognition which saw press coverage on a far grander scale than any previous First Lady, with the possible exception of Eleanor Roosevelt, wife to Theodore Roosevelt from 1905 until he died in 1945. But Jackie Kennedy's place in the political history of the United States extends far beyond that.

It is to her credit that she chose her own path to self-fulfilment, using the position of First Lady to support good causes, to apply her own talents, to identify with her family and the wider public and to campaign for the preservation of public and historic buildings. She became a fashion icon, a cultural ambassador for the United States and a woman devoted to family, her children and to the office with which she was associated.

Born to Wall St stockbroker John Vernou Bouvier III and Janet Lee Bouvier, a socialite of Irish descent, Jacqueline's family tree is covered with French, Scottish, and English branches. Brought up in the Catholic faith, on March 3, 1933 she acquired a younger sibling, Caroline Lee who became an interior designer and public relations executive. Childhood was marred by their father's alcoholism and various affairs which drove their parents apart in 1936, a divorce following in 1940 with great publicity and attention from the press.

Jacqueline had started school in 1935 and was a good pupil but frequently mischievous. She was described by a teacher as "clever, very artistic and full of the devil" before her headmistress impressed upon her the importance of being well behaved. Her mother remarried on June 21, 1942 and would have two more children with her husband, Standard Oil magnate Hugh B Auchincloss. It was he who eventually got Jackie her first job as a receptionist with the *Washington Times-Herald*.

> "Jacqueline had started school in 1935 and was a good pupil but frequently mischievous."

ABOVE: A pleasing and informal picture of Jackie and John Kennedy after their marriage on September 12, 1953.
(Toni Frissell/Library of Congress)

JACKIE

ABOVE: Age six, Jacqueline Bouvier poses for a delightful picture with her dog in 1935. (David Berne/JFK Presidential Library)

church in Rhode Island and 1,200 guests celebrated what was hailed as the reception of the year at Hammersmith Farm.

The next seven years saw JFK rise to the Senate, sharing his campaign as he fought and won the nomination for Democratic Party contender for President before gaining the top job in November 1960. That story has been told in the previous chapter, along with the impressive ascent of this remarkable couple who the world would come to know as the 35th presidency of the United States. It meant a new title for Jacqueline, one for which there was no written script.

A NEW JOB

The title 'First Lady' was first used in a formal sense when describing Harriett Lane, the cousin of bachelor James Buchanan who preceded Abraham Lincoln as President from 1857-1861. It referred to her social responsibilities at the White House, providing food, arranging informal parties, and organising events on the social calendar. The use of that title for a President's wife slipped into only general reference and was not formally used until the 20th century, where it has now become common for identifying the President's wife. With some saying that it cannot surely be long before there is need of a 'First Man', husband to a woman President.

Either way, there is no formal guidebook to the role which has, over time, been crafted according to the expectations of the age and of society and for which there has been no required activities. Just before World War One, President's Harding's wife Florence

The new social circle into which Jackie was suddenly tipped did little to ease her out of her tendency toward withdrawal and a sense of isolation which some interpreted as a sensitive and insecure nature. Compromised perhaps by being moved into different households, each with its own identity from which she felt excluded, friends would observe that it was that which made her determined to chart her own course in life and not be too reliant on uncertainties around her.

Jackie's new home was the Merrywood estate in Mclean, Virginia, time there was shared with Hammersmith Farm, Rhode Island, together with visits to other houses in New York and out on Long Island. Her stepfather provided well for her material needs with a secure and stable environment within which her confidence and self-esteem began to rise. After attending a succession of schools, she settled in at Miss Porter's School in Farmington, Connecticut, from 1944 to 1947 where she was able to fully self-identify away from the social pressures of the Auchinclosses.

On returning to Merrywood, her stepfather saw to it that she got the introduction to the *Washington Times-Herald* where she started her first job but when she pressed for a more responsible position, the editor, Sidney Epstein put her out on the street asking witty questions of passers-by. It was around this time that Jackie fell for a stockbroker, Josh Husted and they became engaged before she found him "boring" and called it off.

It was due to the same social orbit as that of the Kennedys that Jackie met JFK in May 1952 and was instantly attracted to him. They appeared to share a not totally dissimilar background, and both had a love of reading, and both were Catholics. At this time, running for the Senate, JFK had little time for the social norms of a developing relationship, but the couple grew very close, and he proposed marriage after his election.

Jackie had been assigned to cover the coronation of Queen Elizabeth II in London, after which she returned to the United States and resigned her post at the newspaper. Their engagement was officially announced on June 25, 1953 and they were married on September 12 where 700 attended the

ABOVE: Jackie became a universal fashion icon with her detailed attention to dress design, as shown in this formal portrait in the Oval Room of the White House. (NARA)

CHAPTER TWO

ABOVE: Jackie puts on a stunning display of haute couture at the inaugural presidential ball on January 20, 1961. (NARA)

was the first to vote, to deliver speeches and to openly campaign for women's rights, humanitarian causes and to speak about injustices in society. Eleanor Roosevelt's role as wife of President Franklin D Roosevelt was a self-defined job, to be his "eyes and ears" as he suffered from polio. She became the first in that role to have her own radio show and to write a regular newspaper column, authoring several books as well as being influential on the global stage.

Eleanor's self-selected style and responsibilities supporting her husband as his carer defined a new way in which women of her position could connect with the wider world into which they were pitched by circumstances. In some respects, the engaged and active life she epitomised equated well with the emancipation of women during the wartime years, when 10m women, one-third of all American women of working age, were recruited to the labour market, to munitions factories and jobs vacated by men called to arms. To serve, even as carer to a husband with disabilities seemed a natural reflection of American society as a whole in a time of national crisis.

However, during the post-war years from 1945 to 1961, the role fell back on the homebuilding qualities traditionally assumed to be the function of the First Lady. Both Bess Truman and Mamie Eisenhower were in lockstep with a return to traditional, conservative ways of living, a 'Mom and apple pie' life where women were once more returned to kitchens and homemaking, vacating jobs for demobbed servicemen. These wives fulfilled the expected roles of playing hostess at parties and patronising charities. It became very different when Jackie Kennedy moved in to the White House.

Not that Jackie needed advice or the counsel of the wise to understand her new role at the dawn of a changing decade. Instead of assuming a traditional role as the nation's leading housewife, homemaker, and party hostess, she drew on her own talents and skills to support the Office of the President. There were no protocols to follow and the ways in which the First Lady defined her position, while collecting a wide range of activities in support, was a self-defining role. For Jackie there was no supporting cast of advisers. Not until 1977 would there be an Office of the First Lady with its own staff located in the East Wing of the White House.

The task was almost unique, being the third youngest First Lady in the White House and, at a mere 31 years of age, the first of the 'silent generation', defined as those born between 1928 and 1945. Observers noted immediately that the Kennedys would be part of the age of media-savvy politicians playing down grand gestures and passionate commitments. Instead, epitomised by the way Jackie ran things, there would be an elegant, modestly understated approach to high office with little evidence that they had not anticipated this role for their entire lives to that point.

For the public, Jackie became a fashion trend-setter and played to that attraction for American women by hiring Oleg Cassini as her couturier who she called her "Secretary of Style" which elevated his own already considerable standing in the world of dress design. His mandate was simple, and by his own definition, to provide the First Lady with "naturalness, understatement, exposure and symbolism", possible and primarily he would say because of her "beauty."

Emphasising strong geometric lines and exotic fabrics, he matched style of form with pillbox hats, body clothing meticulously

> **"For Jackie there was no supporting cast of advisers. Not until 1977 would there be an Office of the First Lady with its own staff located in the East Wing of the White House."**

ABOVE: Jackie with Indira Ghandi, the future Prime Minister of India. (US Embassy to India)

tailored and fitted with oversized buttons and boxy jackets. In all, Cassini would provide Jackie with 300 outfits, the first of which she wore for her appearance at the inaugural ball in January 1961. The Design Museum in London, England, named that as one of the 50 most influential dresses ever designed. The acclaim she received for his designs and styles reflect well on Cassini himself, who never looked back as he was awarded numerous honours, not least of which was for his humanitarian work as an extramural activity.

PRESERVATION ORDERS

Without a formal staff, Jackie employed a press secretary, Pamela Turnure, who was working for JFK as a receptionist and would remain close to the First Lady throughout the rest of her life. After JFK's assassination she managed his administrative papers which was later funded by Aristotle Onasis. Along the way she also took Jackie's eye for interior design and opened her own consultancy in New York. Rumours that she had been a long term lover of JFK since 1958 were never verified and a book containing those allegations was challenged when it was published in 1997 under the title *The Dark Side of Camelot*.

One of Jackie's purposeful definitions of role was to present herself as a loving mother and family woman supportive of her husband in his high office. That was expected by a lot of American women in 1960 and it was emblematic of the time. But she took that and weaved within it a passionate love of history and architectural style, planning, and managing the restoration of the White House and helping to set up the National Endowment for the Arts, never realising her ambition to found a Department of the Arts.

ABOVE: Jackie with the horse Sardar, a gift from Muhammad Ayub Khan following her goodwill trip to Pakistan. The First Lady had a great love of horses. (JFK Library)

> "For the public, Jackie became a fashion trend-setter and played to that attraction for American women by hiring Oleg Cassini as her couturier."

Restoration of the White House was long overdue. Jackie had visited it in 1941 and had received a tour from Mamie Eisenhower before the Kennedys moved in. She was appalled at the lack of historical continuity, the state of the drab and unappealing décor and at the general condition of the building. Using the extraordinary skills of socialite Sister Parish, she started work on the family quarters first, installing a new kitchen, putting in additional rooms for children and improving the general decoration together with wall and soft furnishings.

With the original budget exhausted, she then turned to the formal and official rooms with funds not immediately available. For advice she turned to Henry du Pont, a horticulturalist and collector of fine art around which he developed a sympathetic style of compatible furniture pieces. To pay for all this, Jackie published a guide book

ABOVE: Jackie shares a family vacation at Hyannis Port with her dogs, among which is Pushinka, a pup from Strelka, one of two dogs sent into space and a gift from Khrushchev. (JFK Library)

CHAPTER TWO

to the public rooms and money from that went on restoration and redesign. Rachel Lambert Melton took charge of redesigning and replanting the Rose Garden as well as the layout of the East Garden. It would be renamed the Jacqueline Kennedy Garden after her husband's assassination.

Throughout, Jackie saw the White House as reflecting good taste and superior quality, providing a stage for presenting the best of American culture, design and style to the numerous guests which would visit and sometimes be entertained there. It was a revolution in the way the First Lady saw that role and the work she did there changed the perception of the Presidency appreciably, defined by the appearance of the place and her influence on presentation.

Previously, President's and their wives had moved furniture in and out on a selective basis, mixing periods which resulted in an uncoordinated display without clear design or a distinct and identifiable style. The confusing appearance offended Jackie's eye for clear design and compatible furniture pieces. She played a significant role in putting these furnishings in the ownership of the Smithsonian Institution which would prevent future occupants from adding or removing items of their own volition. Some had removed items claiming they were their own property.

To formalise all the changes and improvements she made, Jackie set up the White House Historical Association and the Committee for the Preservation of the White House, and later the White House Endowment Trust and the White House Acquisition Trust. These bodies would secure the house and its contents under the

ABOVE: An informal photograph of Jackie and her husband alongside the traditional tree in the White House prior to Christmas 1962. (NARA)

ownership of the people as a national asset and a memorial to the history of the Union. To oversee all these activities, in March 1961 she set up a new position and appointed a curator, Lorraine Waxman Pearce, who had written the guidebook and overseen much of the restoration. She resigned a year later to teach art, but that position remains in place today.

The White House restoration programme got the attention of the media and on February 14, 1962 Jackie hosted a live TV tour of the building with CBS news presenter Charles Collingwood. She explained her commitment by declaring that "I feel so strongly that the White House should have as fine a collection of American pictures as possible. It's so important… the setting in which the presidency is presented to the world, to foreign visitors. The American people should be proud of it. We have such a great civilisation. So many foreigners don't realise it. I think this house should be the place we see them best."

Jackie's love of historic architecture had drawn her attention to plans for redevelopment of Lafayette Square, an area in Washington DC which includes the White House and several federal office buildings. Her attention and concentrated efforts helped save Renwick Square which is now absorbed into the Smithsonian Institution and preserved for the nation.

A ROVING AMBASSADOR

Jackie's cultural and language skills made her an ideal candidate for assisting JFK with international visits and hosting foreign guests. Fluent in French, Spanish, and Italian she had a comprehensive knowledge of their histories and shared a common respect for heritage. Actively engaged with supporting foreign trips, for her first visit to France as First Lady she had a small TV film shot on the White House lawn and

ABOVE: Enjoying a relaxing horse ride, Jackie with John F Kennedy Jnr, accompanied by Caroline Kennedy on her own horse. (JFK Library)

> "Jackie Kennedy's life after her husband's assassination is replete with reflections and reminiscences of one brief, shining moment where she herself referred to those precious few years as comparable to King Arthur's Camelot."

ABOVE: A formal portrait of Jackie with her husband, John Jnr, and Caroline on the veranda of their home at Hyannis Port. (Cecil W Stoughton)

during her stay she impressed with her fluent use of the French language. Parisians were so enamoured with her that JFK was heard to jest: "I am the man who accompanied Jacqueline Kennedy to Paris!"

During the heated mini-summit in Vienna in June 1961, Premier Khrushchev extended his hand to JFK before pulling it back and redirecting it to Jackie first. The Soviet leader sent her a puppy named Pushinka, an offspring of Strelka, one of the two dogs that had been recovered from a space mission. Many aides and assistants would testify to her talent in crafting conversation and dialogue with officials from the countries she visited during her time as First Lady, a valuable asset when political debate got heated and light relief was welcomed. Her Spanish language skills were particularly useful in discussions with Latin American leaders.

Jackie had three children, Caroline, John Jr and Patrick after a miscarriage in 1955 and a stillborn baby girl the following year which was never named but which Jackie always referred to as Arabella. Caroline was born on November 27, 1957 and became an author, attorney, and a diplomat, also serving as US ambassador to Japan. John Jr was born on November 25, 1960 and worked as a lawyer, journalist and a magazine publisher but was killed when his private plane crashed on July 16, 1999. Patrick was born by caesarean section on August 7, 1963, the first child born to an incumbent President. He died two days later of hyaline membrane disease for which there was no treatment at that time.

The story of Jackie Kennedy's life after her husband's assassination is replete with reflections and reminiscences of one brief, shining moment where she herself referred to those precious few years as comparable to King Arthur's Camelot. She said that many times JFK would play the title tune from the musical of that name before going to bed and that became a recognisable epithet for the 'Camelot' era.

It took more than a year for Jacqueline to begin the process of rebuilding her life, but long periods of depression and self-dejection followed her. All the while, Robert Kennedy was a pillar of support for her until his own assassination in 1968 returned those bouts of darkness and mental strife.

Jacqueline remarried, on October 20, 1968 becoming the wife of her long-serving friend and confidante Aristotle Onassis where she began working for the Newport Restoration Foundation preserving historic buildings and houses of the colonial era. With numerous residences and a horse farm in New Jersey, Jacqueline shared time with JFK's younger brother Edward Kennedy.

Aristotle Onassis died on March 15, 1975 but Jacqueline was never to get an equitable share of his vast estate due to Greek law which saw her settle for $26m and write off further claims. Returning to publishing where she had started, she worked with Viking for a while and managed Jeffrey Archer's novel *Shall We Tell the President* before being hired by Doubleday, all the while maintaining contact with the Democratic Party and advising the Clintons on life in the White House.

Diagnosed with cancer after a routine medical examination following her fall from a horse, she died on May 19, 1994 surrounded by her children. President Clinton gave a eulogy at her funeral, and she was buried in Arlington National Cemetery, Washington DC, a city from where she had once played such a significant, some would say magnificent role supporting her first husband in his role as President. Never constrained, Jackie followed her own path and led her own life, which never really came together again after the death of John Fitzgerald Kennedy.

ABOVE: After Jack's assassination, Jackie maintained close contact with the Democratic Party and frequently accompanied future Presidents and their wives, she is seen here with Hillary Rodham Clinton, the wife of President Bill Clinton in 1993. (White House)

CHAPTER THREE

THE BELTWAY BOYS

Before the inauguration speech, the transition period in the political management of the United States between the Presidential election and the inauguration itself is always fraught with action, endless meetings to find missing cabinet positions and haste – JFK had only 73 days to get it all right. The transition team for the incumbent administration works either intensively or sometimes with little enthusiasm, especially when it involves bringing in an opposing party to the one leaving office. It can be a tense time, with the mood set largely by the state of play between parties.

Eisenhower's Republican government was standing down after two consecutive terms in office and hopes of the Vice President, Richard Nixon, carrying a refreshed baton into the White House had been dashed by the election. On this occasion, Eisenhower had insisted on a congenial transfer of power, which is by no means always the case, and the Kennedy team responded by working with them to get briefings over policies and programmes exchanged productively. It was in these meetings that the incoming teams learned for the first time all the internal nuances of agreements and proposals extended to organisation, agencies, and government departments – sometimes to other countries.

A good relationship here is vital for continuity of governance and the preservation of integrity, factors which bore heavily as Kennedy took breath after the election. Seeking respite at Palm Beach, just before leaving his Hyannis Port home he dined with friends and listened to their disparate views, only for them to open the papers the following morning and read the decisions he had already made about positions they had so heatedly discussed over dinner the previous evening. That was the way with this man – give free speech full airing and wait for the response when the sealed decision was publicly declared.

The first formal meeting between Kennedy and Eisenhower took place in early December 1960 and after a deep discussion lasting 75 minutes they walked arm-in-arm to the cabinet room where a broader discussion could begin. There was much that had to be handed over, not least the keys to the nuclear arsenal contained as codes and ciphers carried inside a large case looking like a physician's bag of medical tools with a small communications

"Eisenhower had insisted on a congenial transfer of power, which is by no means always the case, and the Kennedy team responded by working with them to get briefings over policies and programmes exchanged productively."

ABOVE: President Eisenhower (left) walks with Jack Kennedy. The transition between administrations was a time-consuming affair as the incoming teams received briefings on the state of the nation. (White House)

BELTWAY BOYS

ABOVE: J Edgar Hoover ran the FBI as its director from 1937 until 1972 and accumulated large files on key figures in and outside government apparatus, a key asset in keeping opponents of the presidency at bay. (FBI)

tunnels affording ready access from restaurants and eating dens to hurry politicians to their voting lobbies when the session bells rang. It was a separated environment from the rest of the Union where states administered their own budgets, some larger than most other countries. But it was accountable, at the polling booth more frequently than that provided by most democracies, and for that reason US politicians and Presidents were particularly aware of approval ratings.

Voted into power by an electorate divided on domestic and foreign policy issues, the margin for President had been the narrowest of the 20th century. Staunchly committed to his New Frontier policies, and little veiled by an allusion to the ideals of the American West, Kennedy struck deep into the core of most citizens by lifting partisan issues to a high plane and uniting common cause with what most people were concerned about – safety, national security, a better life through economic growth and health care.

For many it had been a vote of faith in a better future and expectations were high that Kennedy was the President who could provide that. But it proved more difficult than anticipated to put these reforms into practice, the traditional ways of securing a complacent and conservative path avoiding painful policy swings obstructing early bills in Congress. At the beginning of the Kennedy Presidency the Democrats held the Senate and the House of Representatives.

During Kennedy's term in office Congress passed an oil pollution prevention act to protect US coastlines, a foreign assistance act separating military from non-military assistance programmes and several welfare acts. Most would be left undone as the challenges posed by Soviet intransigence and security

antenna protruding. This was a recent addition to the President's inventory of items never to leave his reach and Kennedy would receive a direct brief on it from Eisenhower the day before he was inaugurated.

Unlike many of his predecessors, and some of his successors too, JFK and his brother Robert came to the highest office as new men to Washington politics, each perhaps a little naive as to what would be expected – in manipulating a way through the maze of intrigue, obfuscation, deals and decisions made inside the Beltway, the I-495 ring-road that encapsulates the city and the buildings where decisions about national affairs governing the separate states of the Union are deliberated over and decided upon. Despite JFK's experience as a Senator, this would be very different and the challenges that met the 'Beltway Boys' (as they were called) were daunting.

POLLS AND A PERSONAL LIFE

Inside the Beltway, things were contained within the secret world of government, interconnected buildings, subterranean

ABOVE: Attorney General Robert Kennedy (right) meets with J Edgar Hoover (centre) and President Kennedy. A close relationship existed between these three men. (White House)

www.keymilitary.com **21**

CHAPTER THREE

threats brought increasing pressure for time and action. But the achievements in many areas of foreign policy and the transformation of defence doctrine to place constraints on the use of nuclear weapons were profound in securing less reliance on their use.

Over time, Americans were generally supportive of the President's actions, with higher than expected approval ratings showing their belief that events had crowded his carefully planned management of international events and that missed solutions were really no fault of his own. The press played its part in projecting a view of the Kennedy administration that was, however, somewhat at variance with reality.

In fact, there was little orderly about the President's life and the commotion of a poorly coordinated lifestyle echoed around the White House. At the time, very little of his driven urge for a high lifestyle, attractive women and questionable moral practices were considered to be the proper business of the electorate. In a later age this pattern of behaviour would appear totally unacceptable.

The image of JFK as a clean-living, home-loving family man had been carefully crafted and honed to perfection long before he stood for office, but in times of stress his excesses were raised to new heights by the crises over Berlin and Cuba, events of 1961 and 1962 which would preoccupy the public gaze. Behind all this was a very different man for whom excesses and indiscretions were known to only a few, albeit however to an increasingly wider audience toward the end of his life.

Defined by the predilections and social norms of the age, Kennedy's philandering was of no great import to the population at large, although political opponents attempted to use rumour as an engine for controversy over his suitability for such high office. Neither was there great interest

> "JFK and his brother Robert came to the highest office as new men to Washington politics, each perhaps a little naive as to what would be expected."

from the media, who did not consider such activity newsworthy or of sufficient concern. 'Public interest' expose was not yet a byword for profiteering on human failings. But such activity by bearers of this high office was certainly not exclusive to Jack Kennedy.

President for only two years before he died of a heart attack in 1923, Warren G Harding had an affair with his mistress Nan Britton who made great profit from it in a book she wrote exposing all the lurid details. Probably unknown to her at the time, Harding had another lover, Carrie Fulton Phillips whose family kept the entire affair secret until 2014 when their racy love letters were finally published. Only when society deemed it acceptable to offer judgement did it become 'newsworthy'.

Discretely avoided in polite conversation, the extramarital affair that President Franklin D Roosevelt had with Lucy Mercer during World War One sustained a physical relationship to the time of his death on April 12, 1945 from a massive heart attack when she was present as he died. Measured against the accomplishments of the man, there was little social shock when the news became more widely distributed.

Nevertheless, on a more pragmatic point JFK's own demands and desires for frequent visits from women smuggled in without any security checks worried Secret Service agents and the protection force assigned to the White House. As many would testify years later, JFK had a very loose regard

ABOVE: Special Assistant David F (Dave) Powers was a personal friend and aide to the Kennedys, holding many secrets about their private lives and frequently called on to arrange female guests for Jack. (White House)

ABOVE: The USS *Sequoia* presidential yacht where time was occasionally spent discussing deep issues and social activities at other times away from the prying eyes of the media or political opponents. (TCI/Wiki commons)

22 JFK – A LIFE REMEMBERED

BELTWAY BOYS

ABOVE: Robert 'Bobby' Kennedy was highly focused and a determined contributor to the task of ridding American institutions of organised crime, but that did not set well with some of the Kennedy associates. (NARA)

White House press credentials allowing him access to following the President on travel, CBS journalist Marvin Kalb saw a young woman hastily entering Kennedy's hotel room. He was quickly tackled to the ground by a security guard, for fear that he had seen something on which he could report. Kalb protested, indignant at the very suggestion that he might do something like that!

Security agents would recall how Kennedy was familiar with the full names of all his closest security guards, gaining their trust and confidence as he operated a ring of associates and high-class contacts. Through them he was able to arrange for clandestine visits both at the White House and other locations where he could be alone with a range of different women, each selected and provided according to his mood and preferences.

Some of his affairs were with well-known women, including his wife's close friend Mary Pinchot Meyer, an artist living in Georgetown, daughter of a wealthy family and wife of Cord Meyer who had a top job at the CIA. She allegedly had a two-year affair with JFK and was frequently a guest at social events where he turned up. She was on the yacht *Sequoia* when he celebrated his 46th birthday in 1963. Only close security personnel and a very few White House staff knew about the affair until much later, when investigation began after she was murdered on October 12, 1964 while walking along the Chesapeake and Ohio Canal towpath.

Very close associates, friends, and fellow travellers in both his political and private life protected JFK from rumour and character defamation. Enemies from disaffected groups and political opponents were kept

ABOVE: In a frame from the film *Seven Year Itch*, Marilyn Monroe flaunts her sexuality in an erotic pose to camera for the 1955 release when she was 29 years old. (Associated Press)

for their warnings, security staff always concerned that such a ready access to the President's private quarters could easily mask an assassin. Especially since there had been repeated warnings that an unusual number of threats had been made by disaffected groups across the United States.

Close guard was kept on dubious aspects of the President's private life to prevent a Trojan horse penetrating the security ring around the White House intent on malicious practice. The FBI and the Secret Service had precedent for guarding these secrets and special consideration was given to preventing news getting out. There was always a suspicion that press reporters would gather information for political opponents, rarely suspecting that it would constitute a 'scandal' story.

The degree to which the press had access to rooms and offices in the White House during the Kennedy years surprises many, an open access as it was too at the Pentagon until 9/11 when the security of US government buildings took on a warlike façade. With

at bay by Bobby Kennedy in particular and by the loyalty of FBI boss J Edgar Hoover who knew where all the metaphorical bodies were buried and could subtly remind troublemakers of how he could bring them down, were they to be too loose-tongued or eager to 'spill the beans'.

A particularly close confidante among the White House staff was aide Dave Powers who had the unenviable task of procuring women for JFK and for arranging their comings and goings, Secret Service agents were primed

> "The achievements in many areas of foreign policy and the transformation of defence doctrine to place constraints on the use of nuclear weapons were profound in securing less reliance on their use."

ABOVE: Jack and Jackie Kennedy hold a party for Dave Powers' 50th birthday in April 1962. (NARA)

www.keymilitary.com 23

CHAPTER THREE

ABOVE: Marilyn Monroe helped Jack Kennedy celebrate his 45th birthday with an erotic rendition of *Happy Birthday*. (NARA)

to warn the President about the First Lady's movements should she inadvisably stumble upon his 'guests'. Agents such as William T McIntyre had to look away when nefarious activities were none too discretely veiled from female staff at the White House, the newly recruited Larry Newman being concerned about the vulnerability of aides and staffers to philandering activity.

Tony Sherman would later explain how he was unimpressed by the sometimes cavalier approach JFK would take to work commitments, relating how the President seemed to take days off at will and without consideration of the consequences. That seemed to him to be at variance with the expectations he had of the President's role. There were misgivings too about JFK's associations with leading social figures, movies stars, cabaret artists and singers, Frank Sinatra and Peter Lawford being high on that list.

From the early campaigning days, JFK and Sinatra struck a bond, sharing a love of fast women, all-night parties, and the high life of American society. It was Lawford who introduced JFK to Marilyn Monroe and Sinatra introduced him to Judith Exner, who was also the mistress of Mafia boss Sam Giancana. Sinatra also introduced JFK to John Roselli, a 'fixer' from Chicago who was involved with a plot to assassinate Castro after he shut down the drinking dens, gambling halls and casinos that had been supported by the Batista government.

There is evidence that Monroe had a one-night stand with JFK after meeting a second time at Bing Crosby's Palm Springs house in March 1962 but there is little indication that it was consummated other than at this one specific encounter. Her most famous involvement with the JFK story occurred two months later on May 19 when she wore a body-hugging cream dress adorned with rhinestones as she performed the most exotic rendition of *Happy Birthday* publicly displayed to a grinning President, ending with her variation of *Thanks for the Memories* and a ton of innuendo. In all likelihood, she always gave her favours to Bobby Kennedy as well, although despite Monroe getting the attention of the FBI who had a very large file on her, there is no direct proof of that.

The connection between Sinatra and the White House was brief, Jackie Kennedy disliking him and banning him from the place while she was there. JFK had grown out of the affable, sleazy lifestyle that he frequently allowed himself to indulge in, as the President he was one of the few 'untouchables' that even this great performer could never equal. JFK had benefitted greatly from Sinatra's patronage, the singer arranging meetings with influential people in the pre-election days, organising dinners with high-flying celebrities and using Jackie's beauty, intelligence, and social charms to draw in admirers who were useful in his political campaigns.

It did little to help their friendship when the FBI tapped into conversations involving Exner's alleged threats to expose the President to connections with the Mafia and purportedly revealed that Sinatra was having an affair with Pat Kennedy, JFK's sister. There were concerns that Bobby Kennedy's success in restraining the activities of the Mafia were losing the mob vast fortunes from illegal activity busted by the Justice Department. The inference being that Sinatra was trying to influence the Kennedy brothers to back off for fear of having their prior associations with the gangs revealed publicly.

HEALTH CRISES

In addition to the back injury he received during combat, Kennedy had a range of physical disabilities and illnesses which were, on several occasions, to affect his ability to work. The usual childhood ailments were common, and Kennedy spent a considerable amount of time in bed before his fifth birthday. The prognosis was not good for, in addition to whooping cough, chicken pox, measles and persistent ear infections, he had scarlet fever for which he was admitted to hospital. After attending The London Clinic in the UK at the age of 30 he was diagnosed with Addison's disease, an endocrine disorder caused by an inadequate supply of hormones.

But it was in the stressful and fatiguing life as President that Kennedy suffered most from

> **"There is evidence that Monroe had a one-night stand with JFK after meeting a second time at Bing Crosby's Palm Springs house in March 1962."**

ABOVE: A close and personal friend of Jack and Bobby Kennedy and wife of a senior CIA official, Mary Pinchot Meyer attends a birthday party for President Kennedy. (Robert L Knudsen/JFK Library)

a series of illnesses and ailments as a variety of medication was prescribed to assuage high fevers, stomach and colon irregularities and was given injections of corticosteroids to combat prostate, urinary tract infections and abscesses. Routinely, he countered severe pain by the application of hot packs and ultrasound treatment. As the first year of his Presidency progressed, the back pains became increasingly troublesome and at the time of the mini-summit in Vienna during early June 1961, he was taking a prescribed cocktail of drugs.

These were administered by Max Jacobsen, one of JFK's three doctors.

Kennedy had visited Jacobsen in September 1960 for an assessment of his ailments. Jacobsen administered high doses of vitamins laced with amphetamines and methamphetamine which induced hyperactivity and severe changes of personality. JFK was only one of several notable celebrities and politicians who used Jacobsen, but the most intense sequence of treatment on Kennedy occurred between late 1960 and May 1962, during which he visited the White House 34 times.

Expressing serious concerns, the US Food and Drug Administration cautioned Kennedy over the cocktail administered by Jacobsen, advising the President to stop the treatment. But Kennedy was keen to continue with them in addition to exercise which he favoured, commenting on the warnings, "I don't care if its horse piss! It works". Robert Kennedy tried to get Jacobsen sidelined but JFK insisted that he needed the treatments and came to rely on their curative powers until he took advice from the other doctors and relied on physical exercise alone.

Off these drugs and the heavy doses of steroids, by the time of the Cuban Missile Crisis in October 1962 his mood swings and fits of depression were sharply reduced and his ability to make serious and rational decisions was notably improved. In time Jacobsen was implicated in dubious and unethical practices and struck off the medical register in 1975. He never practised again.

For all the imperfections in his incomplete life, John F Kennedy remains one of the most admired Presidents of all time. In

> "As the first year of his Presidency progressed, the back pains became increasingly troublesome and at the time of the mini-summit in Vienna during early June 1961, he was taking a prescribed cocktail of drugs."

Gallup's poll of all-time 'greats', JFK comes third behind Martin Luther King and Mother Teresa. In his cabinet assembled over much agonising, detailed discussions with his brother Robert, other advisers and not a small number whose opinion he sought but which were never named, JFK found a supporting cast with more values than the accredited sum of their achievements. It was those men, and probably too the women he knew, who brought some colour and a lot of drama to his turbulent and eventful life. As events unfolded, the Beltway Boys had come of age.

ABOVE: Frank Sinatra was a close friend of the Kennedys, here seen (centre) with President and Mrs Nixon, helping recruit support at Democratic Party conventions. To their right is Giulio Andreotti of the Italian Council of Ministers. (White House)

CHAPTER FOUR

THE FAMOUS FIXERS

During his term in the White House, John F Kennedy received a wide range of expert opinion from advisers and specialists, together with selected officials in his cabinet. He personally made a point of gathering in professional experts, recruiting from industry and from scientific institutions to help him run the country in this decisive decade in human affairs.

The following are a selection of those who figure prominently in the chapters of this publication, others not so much but of equal importance to the bigger picture of events in the Kennedy administration, and some critical to decisions made in the White House and some who ran government agencies and departments, listed in alphabetical order.

ACHESON, DEAN (1893-1971) ADVISER TO THE PRESIDENT

With a background in economics, Dean Acheson provided expert analysis on foreign policy and statecraft, having been the primary architect of President Harry Truman's Cold War strategy and international relations. Responsible for the Truman Doctrine which sought to contain communism and underpinned the 'domino' theory whereby any one country falling to autocracy would bring down another. He also helped craft the Marshall Plan of aid to post-war Europe and the establishment of NATO. Fell out with McCarthy over trials on 'anti-American activities' labelling it a witch-hunt. Crafted policy over how the US should engage with China. Kennedy used Acheson during the Cuban Missile Crisis and he joined ExComm to determine diplomatic mechanisms for resolving the issue. A leading member of a group known as *The Wise Men* who framed post-war US policy, Acheson was granted numerous awards for services to the country and worked to the end. He died of a stroke at his home, found slumped over his desk.

BELL, DAVID (1919-2000) DIRECTOR OF THE BUREAU OF THE BUDGET

With an early career in commerce at the Bureau of the Budget (BoB), Bell joined the US Marine Corps in 1942 and served as an instructor before his honourable discharge in December 1947. For a while he was on the campaign team for the Democratic Party working for presidential nominee Adlai Stevenson. He returned to private life when Harry S Truman lost a re-election campaign to Republican Dwight D Eisenhower in 1952. In January 1961 Bell became Director of the BoB. Formed in 1921 as part of the Department of the Treasury, the BoB moved to the Office of the President in 1939 to forge a

close link with the White House. It was responsible for preparing the President's budget proposal which would be put before Congress for approval. Bell played a critical role in advising Kennedy on the proposed space budgets. In 1970 it became the Office of Management and Budget (OMB). Bell left the BoB in December 1962 and later joined the Ford Foundation advancing social justice around the world.

BUNDY, MCGEORGE (1919-1996) NATIONAL SECURITY ADVISER

From a family engaged in law practice in Boston, Massachusetts and steeped in Republican Party politics, Bundy achieved high scores at Yale University. He ran for local political office but failed before joining the US Army as an intelligence officer. Back in political life from 1945, Bundy became a political analyst close to presidential candidates and was appointed as adviser on national security by Kennedy, who considered him for secretary of state but chose Dean Rusk, an older man to balance his own youth and inexperience. Bundy was considered to be one of Kennedy's 'wise men' and joined the group believing Rusk was not up to the job. Bundy was crucial in giving Kennedy advice over Cuba and pressed for more involvement in Vietnam, reinforcing that when he served under President Johnson before leaving government in 1966 to become President of the Ford Foundation. Eventually he became a strong opponent of a military solution to Vietnam and in 1979 returned to academic life.

DULLES, ALLEN (1893-1969) CENTRAL INTELLIGENCE AGENCY

The younger brother of John Foster Dulles who served as Eisenhower's Secretary of State, Allen graduated from Princetown University and joined the diplomatic service in 1916. Assigned first to Switzerland, he became part of the Paris Peace Conference to decide the fate of countries after World War One and worked with the Near East Division of the Department of State until 1926 when he joined a law firm. Dulles met with European leaders after serving as adviser on arms limitation controls at the League of Nations, meeting Hitler, Mussolini, and Russia's Maxim Litvinov. During the war he worked for the Office of Strategic Services (OSS), formed to conduct espionage behind enemy lines. From Berne in Switzerland, he passed intelligence information on German V2 rockets to Operation Crossbow, an Anglo-American effort to disrupt their production. Recruited to the CIA, he was in charge of covert operations from 1951 and became the agency's first civilian director in 1952. He left the CIA in November 1961 over policy issues but was appointed to the Warren Commission investigating JFK's assassination.

GILPATRIC, ROSWELL 1906-1996 DEPUTY SECRETARY OF DEFENSE

The son of a New York lawyer, Gilpatric graduated from Yale in 1928 and attended law school where he became editor of their journal. A friend of Nelson Rockefeller and rising rapidly through various law firms, he was schooled in Washington politics and served as secretary of the air force for two years from 1951. From 1956 he worked for the Special Studies Project, a philanthropic Rockefeller organisation defining US opportunities, capabilities and identifying problems the nation might face. One of a very few personally selected by the President,

CHAPTER FOUR

he worked for Kennedy as deputy secretary of defense to McNamara, Gilpatric worked closely with his boss who together formed an alliance of ideas that impressed Kennedy. Gilpatric was crucial in decisions over Berlin and Cuba, proposing a cautious restraint while exuding a strong anti-communist sentiment. Married five times, he was a very close personal friend of Jacqueline Kennedy and is believed to have been her lover for many years, a rumour not denied by either. He left office in 1964.

JOHNSON, LYNDON B (1908-1973) VICE PRESIDENT

Born in poverty to a Texas farming family, working his own way through school, a member of the House of Representatives, then senator and finally vice president and President, Lyndon Johnson was one of the all-time greats in US politics. Shocked by the abject poverty he saw around him,

Johnson pledged his political life around what he would later call his Great Society programme of social reforms. Standing for the 1960 presidential nomination, he was beaten by Kennedy who brought him on board as his running mate, succeeding him as President after the latter's assassination. Johnson provided a balance for the Kennedy administration but was ideologically at odds due largely to the very different social classes from which the two men originated. Johnson provided Kennedy with the experience and political gravitas that came from his ambitious and aggressive use of politics, a ceaseless work ethic and a certainty of purpose that came from fundamental convictions. Johnson did not stand for re-election in the 1968 campaign

KENNEDY ROBERT F (1925-1968) US ATTORNEY GENERAL

An astute member of the Democratic Party's liberal elite, John F Kennedy's brother was eight years his junior and benefitted from the wealthy and politically-engaged family which provided opportunities he used to great benefit. A staunch advocate of civil rights and restrictions on mafia and union influence over local politics, RFK practised law and served as his brother's confidante throughout their lives, especially so during the Berlin and Cuba crises. JFK appointed his brother attorney general, to the fury of organised crime gangs who supported JFK's run for the presidency on the promise than RFK would never fill that office; JFK had used their promises to get pledges of restraint over criminal activities and secure votes. Aligned with human rights and social justice, RFK was against the war in Vietnam and became a lead contender for presidential nomination with the Democratic Party in 1968. After supporting Israel over the six-day war of 1967, he was gunned down by a Palestinian agitator and died a day later on June 6, 1968.

MCNAMARA, ROBERT (1916-2009) SECRETARY OF DEFENSE

The son of a father who fled the Irish potato famine in 1850, Robert achieved high grades in school and at Harvard before working for a firm of accountants. After a brief stint with Price Waterhouse, in 1940 he returned to Harvard where he taught analytical business techniques to Army Air Force officer students. In 1943 he served with the AAF analysing the bomber raids on Japan conducted by Curtis LeMay and introduced the notion of using B-29s for logistical and freight delivery. Joining Ford Motor Company in 1946 he revolutionised their operations by using extensive questionnaires, but employees labelled him a 'Quiz Kid' which he objected to and renamed it 'Whizz Kid'. Rising rapidly, he became the first president of Ford from outside the family on December 9, 1960. Accepting a massive cut in salary he became secretary of defence on January 21, 1961 and became one of the Kennedy's very close family associates, remaining with the Johnson administration until February 28, 1968 after which he became president of the World Bank.

NITZE, PAUL (1907-2004) INTERNATIONAL SECURITY AFFAIRS

Born to German parents and brought up in an academic home, Nitze graduated from Harvard in 1928 and entered investment banking before he was sent to Europe by a brokerage firm. During World War Two he joined government service, hired by James Forrestal who worked for President Roosevelt. From 1944 he helped compile the wartime strategic bombing survey which gave him a profound awareness of nuclear weapons and helped him press for arms controls. In the Truman administration he crafted the 1950 NSC-58 document defining US policy against Soviet communism. Kennedy appointed him assistant secretary of defence for

International Security Affairs and in 1967 he became secretary of the navy, and a key member of strategic arms limitations talks in the 1970s, President Reagan's chief arms negotiator in the 1980s and adviser to the first Bush presidency. He is regarded as the prominent US arms policy shaper of the second half of the 20th century.

O'DONNELL, KENNETH P (1924-1977) WHITE HOUSE APPOINTMENTS SECRETARY

One of the more powerful positions for running internal activities in the White House and for organising the President's formal and informal life, 'Kenny' O'Donnell grew up in family of Irish descent and graduated from high school before joining the US Army in 1942 flying 30 missions as a bomb aimer on B-17s. Shot down over Belgium, he escaped from a prison camp and was awarded the DFC and Air Medal with four oak leaf clusters. After graduating from Harvard, he worked in public relations and retained a friendship forged with Robert Kennedy and joined JFK's staff in 1958. He was taken in to his White House roles from the inauguration day. O'Donnell continued to serve after the assassination of JFK and worked for Johnson, running for local politics twice and losing before serving on the election campaign for Robert Kennedy. Never getting over the loss of both Kennedy's, he took to excessive drinking and died of alcohol poisoning maintaining his insistence that there were additional shots on the day JFK died.

ROSTOW, WALTER (1916-2003) COUNSELLOR, US DEPARTMENT OF STATE

Born to a Russian-Jewish immigrant family named Rostowsky before shortening their name, 'Walt' Rostow was brought up closely following Soviet activities, entering Yale University age 15. He graduated four years later and became a Rhodes Scholar at Oxford University where he befriended Edward Heath and Roy Jenkins, assisting Alistair Cooke reporting on events for the NBC network. During World War Two he worked for the Office of Strategic Services on disruptive action against Nazi forces in Europe and in 1945 joined the division of the State Department studying the strategic bombing offensive, becoming a strong advocate of that campaign, unlike others including Schlesinger who believed that it had had little effect on the war effort. His book *Stages of Economic Growth* was highly regarded by JFK who appointed Rostow as assistant to Bundy. Kennedy found him too preoccupied with a surfeit of ideas and overly confidant about US support for Vietnam. Rostow left office after Nixon became President and his position over Vietnam prevented further government service.

CHAPTER FOUR

RUSK, DEAN (1909-1994) SECRETARY OF STATE 1961-1969

Born and brought up in Georgia, Rusk became a Rhodes Scholar at Oxford and joined the US Army during the war. Senior adviser to Joseph Sitwell, the general in charge of the China-Burma theatre, after leaving the service in 1945 he entered government as a civil servant at the State Department rising high under Dean Acheson. In 1952 he left the government to work with the Rockefeller Foundation where he became president. Kennedy selected Rusk for the top job at the Department of State where he served for eight years, a quiet man who kept his views to himself and rarely asked for opinion. Rusk had worked for the Democratic Party all his life but only got the job when Kennedy's first choice, William Fulbright proved too controversial. Addressed unusually as "Mr Rusk" by JFK, he took over an agency with more than 23,000 staff, twice the size when Acheson ran it. Hawkish over Vietnam, he was unsuccessful in convincing Kennedy to send a large contingent of troops to quell the insurgency from the North.

SALINGER, PIERRE (1925-2004) WHITE HOUSE PRESS SECRETARY

A native of San Francisco, Pierre Salinger was expected to enter a career in music, such was his talent, but after graduating he worked as a journalist from 1941 before joining the US Navy in 1943 and captaining a submarine-chaser in the Pacific. His bravery brought him a medal but after the war he returned to University and studied before becoming a horse racing journalist and a contributing columnist to *Collier's* magazine. After he authored several articles about labour unions, Robert Kennedy hired him as an unofficial adviser. His skill and abilities with the piano brought him to the notice of Jacqueline Kennedy who attracted celebrities and socialites to hear him play. JFK hired him as his press secretary and he ranged freely on the

international stage, talking with Khrushchev in 1962 and receiving a complimentary comment from the Soviet leader. Salinger was at the heart of events during the Cuban Missile Crisis, carefully crafting press statements to avoid unintentional bias or shifting expectations. Salinger won a California Senate seat in 1964 but resigned and became vice president of Continental Airlines.

SCHLESINGER, ARTHUR M (1917-2007) HISTORIAN, WRITER

The need for a special adviser on foreign affairs was enhanced by the priority placed by Robert and John F Kennedy on Latin America and the Caribbean. An academic and graduate from Harvard, Schlesinger spent two years at Peterhouse, Cambridge in the UK where he was a Henry Fellow. During World War Two he worked for the Office of Strategic Services, planning clandestine disruptive action in occupied Europe. From 1946 he lectured at Harvard with a full professorship from 1954 and in January 1961 joined the Kennedy administration. Deeply opposed to the Bay of Pigs attack on Cuba, he argued for restraint and spoke determinedly about his opposition on the grounds that it would "fix a malevolent image" of the United States in the minds of foreigners. Schlesinger resigned after JFK's assassination and wrote a commentary of the President's life in *A Thousand Days: John F Kennedy in the White House*.

STEVENSON, ADLAI (1900-1965) US AMBASSADOR TO THE UN

Born in California but raised in Illinois, Stevenson went to Princeton University then Harvard and entered law, joining a prestigious firm in Chicago. A lifelong member of the Democratic Party, Stevenson entered government as a general counsel and then chief attorney to the agency controlling the alcohol industry. In 1940 he became special assistant to the secretary of the navy and in 1945 worked temporarily for the State Department. Serving as governor of Illinois from 1949 to 1953, Stevenson ran for President in 1952 and 1956 and again, with some reluctance in 1960. Appointed as Kennedy's ambassador to the United Nations, he served from 1961 to 1965. Opposed to the Bay of Pigs, Stevenson managed the flow of diplomatic activity over the Cuban Missile Crisis. He died in London of a massive heart attack while walking with his aide.

WEBB, JAMES E (1906-1992) NASA ADMINISTRATOR

A native of North Carolina, Webb received his Bachelor of Arts in 1928 and served with the US Marine Corps from 1930 to 1932 and then began government service as secretary to Representative Edward W Pou, assisting him as he became aged and infirm. Serving as assistant to attorney Oliver Gardner, he then moved to industry with Sperry Gyroscope as personnel director, then treasurer and later the vice-president. Re-enlisting in the Marines in 1944, Webb planned radar operations for the impending invasion of Japan, but the war ended, and he never saw action. Back in government with the Bureau of the Budget he then worked for Acheson in the State Department before his appointment as administrator of NASA in February 1961. Webb was critical to the Apollo Moon

programme but resigned on October 7, 1968 but remained active in Washington DC. The James Webb Space Telescope is named after him.

WIESNER, JEROME (1915-1994) CHAIR OF THE SCIENCE ADVISORY COMMITTEE

Born in Detroit to an immigrant family from Silesia, Wiesner studied mathematics and engineering at the University of Michigan, working on microwave radar from 1942 and briefly at Los Alamos National Laboratory in 1945. From 1946 he was at the research laboratory of the Massachusetts Institute of Technology (MIT). Obtaining his doctorate in electrical engineering in 1950, Wiesner participated in scholarly academic conferences and was selected by Kennedy to chair the President's Science Advisory Committee. Highly supportive of a space programme to inspire a new generation to enter science and engineering, he was opposed to manned space flight and argued strongly against the Apollo Moon mission model. Wiesner later argued against the indiscriminate use of pesticides in agriculture and was a key figure in the partial test ban treaty of 1963. He left office in 1964 and served as president of MIT from 1971 to 1980.

CHAPTER FIVE

TO THE MOON!

JFK had a seminal role to play in the evolution of America's space programme, setting it alight and creating a goal that would put the first boot prints on the Moon before the end of the decade. The infrastructure in government and industry created to achieve that goal would endure through a succession of evolving policies which would continue through the next several decades and stimulate national space programmes around the world. But the Space Race had been unexpected.

The shock of Sputnik 1 being launched on October 4, 1957 (October 5 in Russia) had stunned the world into accepting the Soviet Union as an emerging superpower. Sputnik 1 was launched several months ahead of its US equivalent Explorer I and further Sputnik launches showed the potential of Soviet rocket power. The events triggered a series of Congressional hearings that for some time in 1958 appeared to dominate the politics of that year. Congress set up the National Aeronautics & Space Administration (NASA) on October 1, 1958.

Responding to concerns over Soviet supremacy, in October 1960 JFK issued a campaign statement on space in which Dr Edward C Welsh said: "control of space will be decided in the next decade. If the Soviets control space, they can control Earth." Kennedy had chosen Welsh to run a task force working on reorganising the Department of Defense. An economist by education and inclination, in 1956 he had chaired Senate air power hearings and was now in charge of JFK's declarations on space.

During the 1960 election campaign, increasing attention was paid to JFK's policies on a wide range of government activities. The 1958 legislation that established NASA also set up the National Aeronautics and Space Council (NASC), a policy-making body. It was chaired by the President and included the secretaries of defence and the Atomic Energy Commission, the NASA administrator, and a range of civilian specialists, one from the government and up to three from outside. Eisenhower became increasingly disenchanted with the 'committee' approach to decision-making and recommended the abolition of the NASC.

At first Kennedy supported that view and planned to abolish the council but after meeting with Lyndon Johnson in December 1960 he reversed that and five days before Christmas announced that the vice president would be chair of the NASC. A report from Jerome B Wiesner of MIT (Massachusetts Institute of Technology) on January 10, 1961 sharply criticised NASA and the way it was managing the civilian space programme. Wiesner questioned the value of putting humans in space at all - NASA planned to put the first Americans in orbit with its one-man Mercury spacecraft –

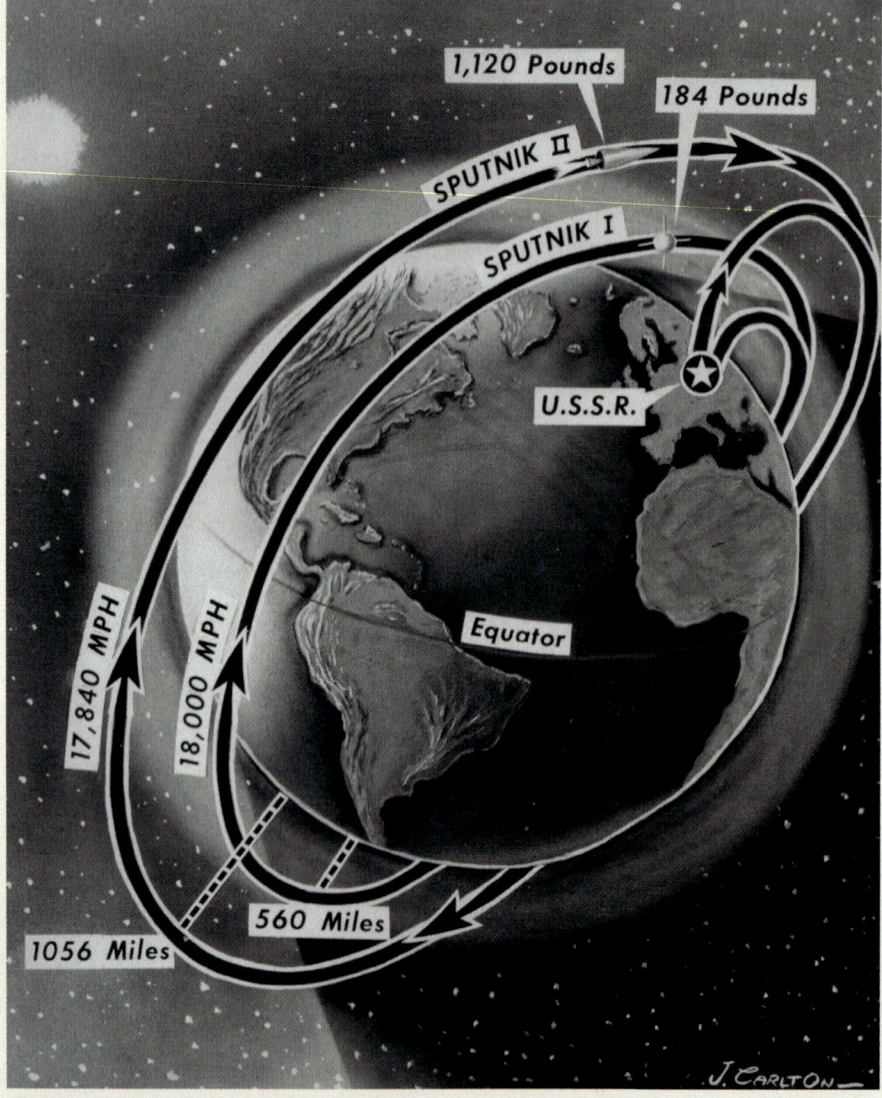

ABOVE: In October and November 1957 Russia embarrassed the Eisenhower administration by launching two artificial Earth satellites before the United States could achieve its own satellite launch. (Novosti)

ABOVE: The Soviet Union used its space 'firsts' to proclaim superiority in the technological race for excellence in science and engineering. (Novosti)

and he proposed cancelling Mercury and cited the extreme political outfall should a disaster befall efforts to get a man in orbit, such an incident inducing 'serious national embarrassment'.

But NASA looked beyond Mercury to a more advanced concept called Apollo with a first flight in 1963, providing a range of capabilities including flights around the Moon by the end of the 1960s. The Apollo spacecraft would be a considerable advance on Mercury. It would rendezvous with other spacecraft, conduct long duration flights lasting two to four weeks and support space walks to practice how to operate outside in the vacuum of space. It would also form the basis for potential landings on the lunar surface using a special module with landing legs.

Eisenhower preferred to wait until the Mercury capsule showed what was possible, what could be done in space and what could not, what value such a programme would have and what it would all cost. He cited the danger of responding to Soviet propaganda with a race for which he saw no value to the United States. However, the public had no breadth of knowledge or certainty about the existing range of military space projects, which by the end of 1960 were considerable and ahead of equivalent Soviet capabilities. Eisenhower did, however, support development of the mighty Saturn series of launch vehicles.

There is little evidence that JFK thought very differently, either in his pre-election statements, speeches, or interviews where he did little except to support the general direction of travel already funded by the Eisenhower administration. Kennedy was undecided about how to position himself on space and the highly visible public attention being given to the astronauts, who had been selected in 1959.

ABOVE: Stamps and memorabilia were produced by the Russians to flaunt their space missions and attract support for their ideological message. (Tass)

When NASA was formed, T Keith Glennan had been appointed its administrator with Hugh L Dryden, as deputy administrator. Glennan handed in his resignation on the election of JFK. But inauguration day came and went without word as to who would run NASA. Glennan resented the lack of contact with the transition team later claiming that: "not one single word or hint of action has been forthcoming from the Kennedy administration." NASA was on hold until the appointment of James E Webb, its new boss from February 14, 1961.

CHOICES AND CONSEQUENCES

As the new administration settled in, NASA girded itself for further scrutiny from Jerome Wiesner. The Mercury programme was well into the operational test phase and moving quickly toward the first attempt at placing an astronaut in space. The Russians had still not conducted a manned operation, although intelligence information predicted an imminent launch, prompting added pressure on NASA for an early Mercury flight. However, the lack of a follow-on manned programme was still of enduring concern, and key to persuading the President to reverse the negative view taken by Wiesner was a viable and affordable plan.

On February 9, 1961 George Low, NASA's manned flight boss, produced a 51-page report. It offered optional ways in which the ambitious mission could be achieved, optimistically indicating that a landing could be achieved by 1970 and grossly oversimplified the necessary steps and technical hurdles to be overcome. A day later, Wiesner convened a two-day meeting of the Space Science Board of the National Academy of Sciences and doubts began to creep in. Nevertheless, the recommendation was for NASA to pursue manned exploration of the Moon and the planets as a national goal worthy of the highest priority. None of those voting on the issue fully understood the magnitude of the work involved.

The first active role played by the President in NASA's affairs came at the urging of David Bell, director of the Bureau of the Budget (BoB). It was his office that would put the final touches to each year's budget proposals sent to Congress. As the old adage has it, 'the President proposes and the Congress disposes'. The outgoing administration presents the budget it would like to see for the following financial year, which in the 1960s began on July 1. But in the opening weeks of a new administration it would review that and make amendments and JFK would mark up any changes he wanted to put before Congress. Very few in the new government knew anything about space or the complexities involved and by their own admission they failed to understand what it was about.

In a critical meeting at the White House on March 22, NASA's Webb, Hugh Dryden,

> "The Russians had still not conducted a manned operation, although intelligence information predicted an imminent launch, prompting added pressure on NASA for an early Mercury flight."

ABOVE: The key figure behind Russia's space achievements was Sergei Korolev, who would remain unknown until his death in 1966 from a botched surgical operation. (Novosti)

www.keymilitary.com 33

CHAPTER FIVE

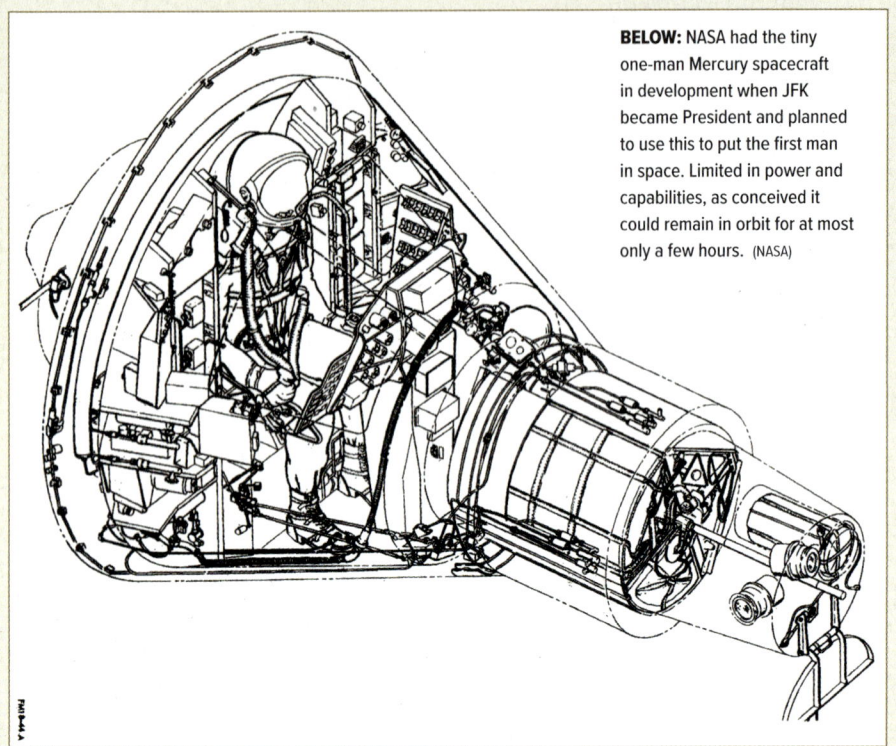

BELOW: NASA had the tiny one-man Mercury spacecraft in development when JFK became President and planned to use this to put the first man in space. Limited in power and capabilities, as conceived it could remain in orbit for at most only a few hours. (NASA)

and Robert C Seamans briefed Johnson about energising the new administration with a forward-thinking plan. Webb pulled a masterstroke when he claimed that the space programme would provide "more viable political, social and economic systems for nations willing to work with us in the years ahead." The meeting closed with the President calling for a written review of those ideas, after which Webb and Johnson went to the Oval Office with Kennedy and exchanged pleasantries. The new NASA boss refrained from his usual inclination to give a long lecture, a tendency which irritated the President who always sought brief, clear, succinct, and fact-based presentations.

Bell summed it up by telling the President: "It seems virtually certain that alternative, surer, and less costly ways of increasing our national prestige in the world scene could be developed." Declaring that the amount of money required for the total programme culminating in a Moon landing would be out of proportion to the benefits. In other words, there were better ways to spend the money, which as calculated by Low in 1960 would amount to $700m for each of 10 years.

Wiesner said he could not support Apollo.

The decision made by the President was to give NASA more money for the big Saturn booster programme but none for Apollo and deferral of a Moon decision until proposals for the 1963 budget were discussed toward the end of that year. In making this judgement, JFK passed over major decisions on the future of the space programme. In reflections much later, Webb said he was aware that Kennedy had many problems to deal with and that NASA was not very far up his list. Politically savvy, Kennedy wanted to defer any serious consideration over long-term space policy until more pressing matters had been dealt with.

Kennedy had been made aware that the Russians were likely to launch a man into

BELOW: The seven Mercury astronauts were selected in April 1959 with the task of flying the Mercury spacecraft. Left to right: Malcolm Scot Carpenter, Gordon Cooper, John Glenn, Virgil 'Gus' Grissom, Walter 'Wally' Schirra, Alan Shepard, and Deke Slayton. (NASA)

ABOVE: On January 30, 1961, Kennedy met with newly selected NASA boss James Webb who had been appointed as the new administrator of the government's civilian space agency tasked with making the US 'pre-eminent in space'. (NASA)

> "While final preparations were underway at the Soviet Baikonur launch site for the flight of Yuri Gagarin, JFK went to bed on the night of April 11 saying that in the event it happened he did not want to be woken."

orbit any day. Faced down by the prospect of another Soviet 'first' to equal that visited upon his predecessor by Sputnik 1, JFK was well aware of the political outfall from another Soviet space spectacular. More so since the inability of the Eisenhower administration to get a satellite up before the Russians had been a campaign issue for Kennedy.

The approach at NASA had been cautionary and a manned ballistic flight carrying Alan Shepard could have been launched on March 24, 1961. However, NASA wanted more tests with yet another unmanned flight but some within the NASA community opposed such caution and warned of the impending threat from a Soviet pre-emption. After all, a bleeping ball had nothing on the excited voice of a human from outer space and the White House girded itself for another national embarrassment. Had an astronaut been on board, NASA would have put the first man in space. The future would have been different.

On the evening of April 11, the CIA alerted Kennedy to a Russian flight as early as the next day and Kennedy's press secretary Pierre Salinger prepared a statement. As early as April 3, Edward R Murrow, head of the US Information Service (USIS) had sent a memo to Bundy recommending that, in the event of a Soviet catastrophe, the President should express his "deep regret and distress" at the shocking news. But if successful it also advised US embassies around the world to encourage statements of concern that the Soviets should have so little regard for human life!

While final preparations were underway at the Soviet Baikonur launch site for the flight of Yuri Gagarin, JFK went to bed on the night of April 11 saying that in the event it happened he did not want to be woken. In Baikonur it was 11.07am on the morning of April 12 when the launch occurred but in Washington DC it was only 1.07am. The CIA and the intelligence apparatus monitored communications from the Russian spacecraft and the TV signal coming down to Soviet ground stations as Gagarin made his single orbit of the Earth. It was several hours before Soviet news channels announced the momentous event to the Russian people.

ABOVE: Throughout 1961, the rocket team working under NASA's Wernher von Braun put together a plan for several highly advanced launch systems capable of sending men to the Moon. (NASA)

ABOVE: With little warning from US intelligence sources, on April 12, 1961 the Russians put Yuri Gagarin into space and beat the Americans, all the more embarrassing because Kennedy had criticised the preceding Eisenhower administration for allowing the Soviets to get ahead. (Novosti)

CHAPTER FIVE

ABOVE: Read by local workers at the NASA Marshall Space Flight Center, the *Huntsville Times* proclaims another 'first', putting America further behind in the space race. (Author's archive)

Responding to a torrent of concern and calls for action to leapfrog Soviet space accomplishments, Kennedy convened a meeting late on that same Friday and took the unprecedented step of inviting *Time Life* journalist High Sidey to sit in. Aware of the public reaction, Kennedy trusted Sidey and hoped that in his coverage he would inject awareness that the President was actively mobilising a response.

Late in the afternoon, before the meeting at the White House, Webb, Dryden, Sorensen, and Bell accompanied by staff member Willis Shapley, Wiesner and Welsh had met to discuss the situation. The possibility of a Moon mission was broached by Sorensen. Dryden thought that it was such a phenomenal and audacious undertaking, calling for so much new technology that it was just possible for the US to beat the Russians to a lunar landing. He would recall thinking that this was the sort of goal that would get the interest of the President.

Wiesner had already prepared Kennedy for that Friday evening meeting with a

To the vast majority of the American population the news was a shock. Nobody had prepared them for this possibility. At a press conference that day Kennedy put on a confident face and articulated the great benefits that would come to science and the nation by consistent support for the space programme. He also began to identify other areas where America could make great progress, perhaps in a more direct way such as desalinisation of the oceans to provide drinking water for all people on Earth.

On this day, a scheduled meeting of the House space committee convened to appoint Johnson head of the Space Council. Chairman Overton Brooks expressed the views of a nation when he asserted: "We ought to make a determination that we…are going to be first." It was a message echoed by Congress which called for a crash programme already defined by Republican James Fulton when he suggested that the US should "publicly say that we are in a competitive space race with Russia and accept the challenge." The pressure was on for a response to calm the nation, to satisfy the American people.

"I DON'T CARE IF IT'S THE JANITOR!"

On March 24 Seamans and NASA's George Low had been subject to intense pressure from the House space committee to accelerate the manned effort, with Low being pushed hard as to whether a Moon landing could be achieved by 1967 – the 50th anniversary of the Russian revolution. Low believed it could be achieved, subject to a major effort and a lot more money, and that it was a 'matter of national policy'. This was three years in advance of the earliest previously cited date and that only possible with the increase Kennedy had already refused, declining funds for Apollo.

"Kennedy had approved the invasion of Cuba at the Bay of Pigs on a plan put together by the Eisenhower administration and orchestrated by the CIA and Cuban exiles."

ABOVE: On May 5, 1961, Alan Shepard rode the tiny Redstone rocket in his Mercury spacecraft on a ballistic flight lasting a mere 15 minutes to show that America's manned flight programme was on track and would soon put its astronauts in orbit. (NASA)

briefing paper identifying advantages with satellites, but Sorensen prompted Wiesner to draft a second memo, generally supportive of the accelerated booster programme. When Kennedy joined the meeting he put Sidey at the head of the table to ask questions. Sidey noted that "Kennedy was very anguished…kept running his hands through his hair, tapping his front teeth with his finger nails, a familiar nervous gesture." Kennedy had reached a pivotal moment and intoned the meeting with a hint of exasperation, some believing that he now realised what had slipped from his grasp during both the campaign and in denying NASA a funded start on Apollo. He ended the meeting by declaring: "If somebody can just tell me how to catch up. Let's find somebody – anybody! I don't care if it's the janitor over there…there's nothing more important."

Before the March 24 meeting, Kennedy had approved the invasion of Cuba at the Bay of Pigs on a plan put together by the Eisenhower administration and orchestrated by the CIA and Cuban exiles. As the opening of the invasion, on April 15 American warplanes began bombing airfields on Cuba with the exiles and other US personnel dressed in similar clothing going ashore at the start of a US-led coup to overthrow Castro. However, within days the operation was recognised as being a total and highly embarrassing failure.

ABOVE: President Kennedy greets Alan Shepard and acknowledges the work still to be done while presenting a medal to the first US astronaut to reach space. (White House)

By April 19 Kennedy was, according to Sorensen "anguished and fatigued…in the most emotional, self-critical state I have ever seen him. He cursed not his fate or advisers but himself," he added that "Kennedy's anguish and dejection were evident to people around him." Added to which, the physical stress of his periodic bouts of severe pain brought on by the lasting effects of his wartime injury played to his sense of frustration and the deeply consequential challenges which lay ahead.

Kennedy's stressed dejection spilled across to the family, Robert Kennedy appealing to attendees at a meeting that day: "All you bright fellows. You got the President into this. We've got to do something to show the Russians we are not paper tigers." Combined, the Russian manned flight and the failed invasion of Cuba wore heavily on the President. The Bay of Pigs was a fiasco but the connection to the space race proved critical. April 19 proved to be the low point in the unfolding saga and a seminal turning point in the Kennedy administration, not least too for the President himself.

It had been a cold night with temperatures dipping down to 5°C (41°F), hardly rising at all as dawn broke around 6.30am. Nursing acute back pain, Kennedy took an early morning stroll with Ted Sorensen, sauntering out through the columned portico of the White House and on to the still damp south lawn. Past the trees and shrubs to either side, across the fountain and toward the Mall, their gaze wandered to the Washington Monument. Searing into the sky it caught Sorensen's eye and he mused that it looked as though it were a finger pointing to space.

The loss of faith he exuded in his own decision to approve the Eisenhower plan and his handling of the Russian space coup weighed heavily on Kennedy and set a gloom for the rest of that day. The dilemma was that no one knew exactly what to do.

ABOVE: The President and Jackie Kennedy host a group of astronauts and their family members, grilling them with questions about the potential for manned flights to the Moon. (White House)

CHAPTER FIVE

BELOW: At a cabinet meeting on May 25, 1961, the final decision is made to announce the goal, later that day, to send a man to the Moon by the end of the decade. (NARA)

In the hope of finding an answer, that afternoon Kennedy met with Johnson and Webb to plan a full analysis and directed the vice president to organise that. Johnson asked for a supporting memorandum, drafted by Sorensen, and given to him the following day.

On April 20 Johnson received directions to plan a response to the Gagarin flight which saw a dramatic call for action from Congress. It was clear that the government had a clean sweep of possibilities, politicians of both parties willing to sign a blank cheque, subject to a genuinely plausible plan to eclipse all potential Soviet capabilities.

TO LAND A MAN ON THE MOON

Kennedy's memo to Johnson consisted of one page and reiterated the three options previously defined by supporters of an accelerated programme: do we have a chance of beating the Russians by putting a laboratory in orbit, of sending a man around the Moon or of landing directly on the surface and how much would that cost?

There was urgency. Kennedy wanted to know: "Are we working 24 hours a day on existing programmes? If not, why not? If not, will you make recommendations to me as to how work can be speeded up? Are we making maximum effort? Are we achieving necessary results?" The April 20 memorandum was a wakeup call, Kennedy concluding that "I would appreciate a report on this at the earliest possible moment."

Close associates are convinced that Kennedy had already made up his mind to propose a Moon landing. Absent from any of this, however, was anything other than it being a political attempt to assuage public and Congressional concerns and to treat it as a headline challenge to raise the flag on

ABOVE: Kennedy announces the Moon goal to mixed reaction among Congressional leaders, an uncertainty echoed by the American people in general. (JFK Library)

THE SPACE RACE

hard, and Webb drove one of them to her home, waiting until it abated before letting her out to her house and driving off. Around 2am on the Monday morning the meeting broke up with details ironed out ready for Johnson's signature. It was, said Seamans later, the act of a gallant Southerner that Webb had been so caring to his staff!

With the weather now fine on that Monday morning, May 8, Jacqueline, and the President met Alan Shepard and the other six astronauts out in the Rose Garden. Shepard had flown in by helicopter from nearby Andrews Air Force Base to receive the NASA Distinguished Service Medal, pinned on Shepard's chest by JFK after dropping it and claiming that it had truly gone "from the ground up!"

Back in the Oval Office with his 20 or so guests, it was as though the depression and tensions that had filled the past several weeks had been sloughed off by his personal decision to a fully-fledged commitment. Surrounded by invitees reclining on sofas and chairs, questions came thick and fast as the President engaged with the group, enthusiastically asserting that "look, I want to be first…I want to go to the Moon." In the upbeat exchanges that followed there was a mood of confidence, brimming over with expectation in clear sight that the President had already made his decision but would await the formal protocols of receiving Johnson's. Architect of the Mercury

ABOVE: Kennedy presents the Collier Trophy to astronauts on October 10, 1963, an event attended by Lyndon Johnson, architect of the Moon landing decision. (JFK Library)

the capabilities of a democratic society. JFK was ever mindful of his driving ambition to position America as a banner standard for 'free' societies.

On May 5 Jacqueline joined JFK, Johnson, Bundy, Schlesinger and Admiral Arleigh Burke, chief of naval operations, to watch the launch of the first manned Mercury mission on a TV set in the office of his secretary, Evelyn Lincoln. Tension had been compounded due to a succession of weather delays before Alan Shepard was launched at 2.34pm, propelled to a height of 187.5km (116.5 miles) by a Redstone rocket and recovered from the Atlantic Ocean. It had been just over three weeks since the flight of Yuri Gagarin and Shepard's flight lasted only 15 minutes before he splashed down 487km (302 miles) from the launch pad at Cape Canaveral. Had this flight not gone according to plan it is unlikely that the decision to go to the Moon would have been made.

Late in the afternoon of Saturday May 6, NASA's Robert Seamans met with Webb to begin work on a draft plan for the President's approval, to be delivered the following Monday. Seamans called Webb who agreed to come by and discuss the concerns after dining with Alan Shepard's family, which he left at 9.30pm going straight to join the group. On through the night the secretaries worked typing drafts, seemingly endless revisions, and final pages. It was raining

ABOVE: Von Braun and Senator Kerr break ground on the new Marshall Space Flight Center where the giant Saturn rockets would be designed. (NARA)

www.keymilitary.com 39

CHAPTER FIVE

ABOVE: Kennedy visited NASA facilities on several occasions and here von Braun is hosting the President at Huntsville where debate about the way NASA would send men to the Moon was contested by science adviser Jerome Wiesner. (NASA)

spacecraft, Robert 'Bob' Gilruth thought the impending decision reflected the bold spirit of a young man and that "If he'd been older, he probably would never have done it."

When Kennedy met with senior officials from NASA, the Budget Bureau, and the Space Council on May 10, he had already made up his mind to accept the proposals. Next would be a formal process of having the programme costed and set within the framework of other government programmes but Kennedy had found a way through his dark days, without bringing in the janitor! The main thrust that JFK took from his decision folded into broader and deeper concerns regarding threats posed by potentially hostile nations. Not in a military sense but in communist ideological dogma his administration saw as challenges to free-world democracy.

The public declaration of the Apollo programme as a major drive to put an American on the Moon came during Kennedy's message to Congress on May 25, 1961. He opened by defining the challenges faced by the United States, both militarily and in the face of a tide of "rising people" in undeveloped parts of the world as yet ideologically uncommitted but increasingly embraced by Soviet and Chinese communism. Much of the speech discussed the "contest of will and purpose as well as force and violence – the battle for minds and souls as well as lives and territory."

After declaring his intention to set up an arms control agency, to put additional funding into national programmes for citizen participation in aid projects and engaging with opponents on the world stage, 30 minutes into a 46 minute address he turned to the space programme, summarising the achievement of the first American in space and declaring a bold effort in words that defined the objective as a race in which the only other contestant was Russia:

"First, I believe that this nation should commit itself to achieving the goal, before this decade is out, of landing a man on the Moon and returning him safely to the Earth. No single space project in this period will be more impressive to mankind, or more important for the long-range exploration of space; and none will be so difficult or expensive to accomplish."

Kennedy displayed a nervous uncertainty as he gave his speech. There was a sense of uncertainty and Sorensen would remark that he looked "strained in his bid to win them over." Uncharacteristically, several times Kennedy deviated from the prepared script and would assert later that he felt he was already losing his audience.

On the drive back to the White House, Kennedy remarked to Sorensen that the anticipated applause for his remarks was "less than enthusiastic." While the senior congressional leadership had been primed for the announcement and gave assent, the majority shuffled and even the party heads "inspected their fingernails, brushed their hair back and joined in the almost complete Republican silence." The press was still less enthusiastic although generally supportive while a poll among Americans showed less than half approved. Media reports polarised around their own partisan affiliations, but the trade press acclaimed the decision, serving an industry keen to compete for lucrative new contracts. The scientific community was sceptical.

Congress had been charged with expectation and for a few months there was majority support for the plan. Over the next several months it gave NASA almost all the

ABOVE: With John Glenn to his right, Kennedy inspects the Friendship 7 Mercury spacecraft which had carried the astronaut into orbit on February 20, 1962. (NASA)

THE SPACE RACE

extra money sought by Kennedy, an increase of almost 90% over the amount requested by the outgoing Eisenhower administration. But it is doubtful that many members fully understood what they were signing up to. Funding would continue to increase at an unprecedented pace, NASA getting $3.673bn for 1963 and $5.099bn for 1964.

The detail in NASA's evolving strategy for getting to the Moon is complex and convoluted in its direction of travel. Suffice here to say that Kennedy became impatient with the pace of preparations and constantly urged a faster effort, pushing hard for an attempted landing in 1966. Yet it took more than a year for NASA to finalise how it would carry out the mission and to select the vehicles it required for that. Reflecting a frustration within the White House, on November 20, 1961 Wiesner noted that "none of these critical hardware programs have progressed beyond the study phase." There was a degree of validity to this concern but by the end of the year NASA had decided it needed another manned spacecraft, a two-man Gemini vehicle to practice essential techniques it would employ on Apollo. Webb observed that Kennedy debated whether decisions over new facilities for the rapidly expanding programme "were based on the needs of the program or had political overtones."

It would be mid-1962 before the decision was made regarding how the Moon mission would be conducted. A second new spacecraft, the Lunar Module, would be needed to carry astronauts down to the surface from lunar orbit where the Apollo capsule would wait to bring the crew back home. The rocket used for each Moon mission would be the Saturn V, a developed evolution from the Saturn I on which

> "Close associates are convinced that Kennedy had already made up his mind to propose a Moon landing. Absent from any of this, however, was anything other than it being a political attempt to assuage public and Congressional concerns."

hopes had been pinned for eclipsing Soviet capabilities in spacecraft lifting power.

With the programme maturing, on May 3, 1962 Webb reported to Kennedy on the latest budget estimates and was warned to ensure that nothing was spent beyond funds "that could be thoroughly justified." Kennedy had cautioned Congress that this would be a costly endeavour but in the first 12 months of the commitment the reality of that began to raise serious concerns. Not least to the President himself. Concern about the use of NASA funds to develop a broad-based programme would haunt Kennedy throughout 1962 and into 1963.

But progress was being achieved. On October 27, 1961 the first stage of the Saturn I made a successful ballistic flight demonstrating a lift-off thrust more than twice that of the largest US rocket to date. Three more test shots would fly before a two-stage configuration could provide a 10-tonne payload capacity. On February 20, 1962, John Glenn conducted the first US manned orbital flight followed by Scott Carpenter three months later. America was catching up.

A CHANGE OF HEART

In mid-1962 Kennedy went to see for himself the work under way on the Apollo programme. Accompanied by Johnson, German rocket scientist Wernher von Braun, NASA officials, congressmen and Wiesner, on September 11 he toured the Marshall Space Flight Center where he was shown work on the Saturn I, models of the Saturn V and given a briefing on the mission mode that had been selected. But Wiesner disagreed and openly challenged von Braun's defence of that plan, known as Lunar Orbit Rendezvous (LOR). As von Braun was explaining the details, Kennedy interrupted, saying "I understand Dr Wiesner doesn't agree with this" and called him over.

Webb and Seamans backed up von Braun, but Wiesner argued his case and the discussion became heated. Voices were raised and the press, kept at some distance, picked up on the increasingly loud voices. Annoyed at what he had started and aware that it was now gathering together a press pack likely to make media mischief, Kennedy cut it short: "Well, maybe we'll have one more hearing and then we'll close the books on the issue."

Kennedy then flew to Cape Canaveral to view construction of the expanding facilities before flying to Houston where the

ABOVE: Throughout 1962 and 1963 von Braun's team refined the Saturn series of rocket to provide the means by which Apollo spacecraft would be sent to the Moon, examples of which are seen behind his desk. (NASA)

CHAPTER FIVE

ABOVE: Kennedy gets a close-up view of the Saturn I SA-5 rocket which would soon put up a payload to equal Soviet space capabilities. (JFK Library)

Manned Spacecraft Center was to be built. Addressing a crowd of 40,000 at the Rice football stadium he delivered an impassioned address which moved many, listening on that swelteringly hot, bright day:

"We set sail on this new ocean because there is new knowledge to be gained, and new rights to be won, and they must be won for the progress of all people. But why, some say, the Moon? Why choose this as our goal? And they may well ask, why climb the highest mountain? Why, 35 years ago, fly the Atlantic? Why does Rice play Texas?

"Many years ago, the great British explorer George Mallory, who was to die on Mount Everest, was asked why he wanted to climb it. He said, 'because it is there'. Well, space is there, and we're going to climb it and the Moon, and the planets are there, and new hopes for knowledge and peace are there. And therefore, as we set sail, we ask God's blessing on the most hazardous and dangerous and greatest adventure on which man has ever undertaken."

Flying back to Washington, he diverted to the McDonnell factory in St Louis where it was building the Gemini spacecraft. The first of 12 flights were expected in early 1964 to test techniques essential for Apollo and the Moon landing. Apollo was expected to fly in 1965 or 1966 but critical technologies employed for the Moon missions would be tested and evaluated on these Gemini flights.

Encouraged by signs of real progress, Kennedy fixated on speeding up the attempt and now consistently urged a landing in 1966. NASA knew this was impossible, but Kennedy was aware of the difficulties. Wiesner continued to criticise the LOR mode and was determined to argue the case strongly when it was taken to the meeting promised by Kennedy when he had encountered dissent during his visit to the Marshall facility.

In preparing to defend his position at the impending White House meeting, on October 24 Webb wrote to Wiesner clarifying why the decision had been made. He sent a copy to Kenneth O'Donnell, controller of Kennedy's appointments, suggesting that unless Wiesner disagreed it was unnecessary to request a formal meeting

A characteristic of JFK, having appointed heads of government agencies he was unsettled to the verge of annoyance by cross-agency interference. Wiesner had simply run out of options.

Kennedy was proud of the 'can-do' spirit and used the burden of commitment, personal sacrifice, and determination to succeed as pillars of a robust and successful society led by, and run for, individual citizens. In several speeches throughout his political career, he invoked a sense of inclusivity between the political elite and the majority of the population. Born to high privilege, he espoused the principles of his party – social justice, a welfare net for the disenfranchised and an inclusivity welding broader society to the individual. But he sought to balance that expectation in the citizenry with demands of the individual and the space programme was no exception.

In addressing the audience at Rice University on September 12 he had delivered that in as clear a way as at any other time in his Presidency: "We choose to go to the Moon in this decade and do the other things, not because they are easy, but because they are hard, because that goal will serve to organise and measure the best of our energies and skills, because that challenge is one that we are willing to accept, one we are unwilling to postpone, and one which we intend to win."

END GAME

The Moon landing was planned for late 1967 but there were unanticipated technical challenges, increasing the money it felt was needed to get to that goal. Along with Bell, Shapley, Welsh and Wiesner, on November 21, NASA's Webb, Dryden, Seamans, and Brainerd Holmes met with Kennedy in the White House to thrash out the fiscal 1964 budget which would be put to Congress in early 1963.

As conversation began to unfold, Kennedy discretely switched on the secret audio recording system he had installed in the Oval Office three months previously. Responding to Webb's assertion that the manned Moon programme was one of the agency's top priorities, Kennedy asserted that it was "*the* top priority", adding that "I think we ought to have that very clear…This is important for political reasons, international political reasons…Some of these other programmes can slip by six months, and nothing strategic is going to happen." And emphasising that it was for political reasons alone, Kennedy told the group "I'm *not* that interested in space."

According to Wiesner, JFK sought a different response but could find no other way: "If Kennedy could have opted out of a big space program without hurting the country in his judgement he would have. I think he became convinced that space was the symbol of the 20th century. It was a decision he made cold bloodedly." Where Kennedy had initially mobilised the space resources of the nation in a drive to compete against rigid and autocratic communist regimes, he now saw the space programme as a means of engaging with that opposing ideology and to do so in a manner that would bring the rest of the world along with him.

Kennedy kept alive these prospects and in response to congratulatory messages from the White House on successful

with the President to open the case again. An unambiguous endorsement from the White House was critical as NASA wanted to get a contractor signed up to build the Lunar Module, essential for the LOR mode.

However, during this period Kennedy was deeply involved with the Cuban Missile Crisis, occupied with trying to prevent a major war with the Soviet Union. Webb left it in the hands of O'Donnell to take a position on whether Kennedy would want to sit out a deeply technical discussion on unfamiliar matters over which he lacked the knowledge to make a personal selection. Wiesner declined to force the issue and the matter died right there, batted away by the national crisis gripping the nation.

BELOW: Hosted by NASA's Robert Seamans (left) and Wernher von Braun (centre) on November 16, 1963 Kennedy visited the NASA launch facilities at Cape Canaveral and saw the Saturn I rocket that would help eclipse Soviet successes. (NASA)

CHAPTER FIVE

planetary launches, Khrushchev responded with guarded interest, advising that such cooperation would only occur when disarmament was achieved. Much of the planning for a Kennedy-Khrushchev summit had taken place between the flight of Alan Shepard on May 5 and the public declaration of the Moon goal three weeks later. It did little to change the direction of White House policy on space or the strategy for how that would be achieved and while cooperation had been at the forefront of Kennedy's interest in meeting with Khrushchev which took place in Vienna, Austria on June 3-4, 1961 it failed to realise any potential for imminent change.

The Cuban Missile Crisis of October 1962 did little to dampen enthusiasm for a deal with Russia over the Moon goal, only to encourage Kennedy to use space as a potential softener in relations between the two countries. There was little enthusiasm among the Soviet military leadership, despite Kennedy having proposed a coordinated approach to the unmanned exploration of the lunar surface to save costs. Khrushchev told Kennedy that he had intervened to prevent a race to the Moon because it was "costly and was primarily for prestige purposes."

It is significant that the Russians were explicit in noting the Moon race as a US bid without an acknowledged competitor, Khrushchev repeating how he regarded space exploration as a tool of political propaganda and little else. In the Russian mind-set, they had already won by seeming to have exposed an American sensitivity which, they said, would not have resulted in the public declaration of a landing goal had the US not felt insecure.

PLANETARY PARTNERS?

On September 20, 1963 Kennedy addressed the General Assembly of the United Nations and stunned delegates unfamiliar with the changing mood at the White House. In response to what he had perceived as a softer tone from Khrushchev after the missile crisis of October 1962, Kennedy offered the Soviet Union a cooperative deal that shocked many hardliners in the United States. Political support was eroding in the wake of a succession of US achievements. To Kennedy and many others, it appeared that the US was rapidly overtaking the Soviet Union and had fulfilled the obligation of the 1958 National Aeronautics and Space Act in making America 'pre-eminent in space'.

ABOVE: Brought in during late 1963 to reorganise the manned lunar landing programme, George E Mueller restructured the way Apollo was being developed by establishing an accelerated timeline. (NASA)

The escalating cost of Apollo and supporting rockets such as Saturn was of increasing concern to Kennedy, more so due to the sustained opposition in Congress to further budget increases which were only set to grow as demand for funds soared. Kennedy evaluated the options: deflect further increases by downscaling the schedule, reducing projected budget demands by capping the rise; or letting it run its course and risk mobilising opposition in Congress. Kennedy decided to engineer a way through by falling back on the division of responsibility offered by the prospect of a joint venture with the Russians.

Perhaps surprisingly, Webb was not averse to the idea, but many at NASA and in the US Air Force with which the space agency had close ties, saw this as a default orchestrated by the White House to renege on set goals. And there was much at stake to unsettle the industry, where considerable corporate investment had followed government contracts built on expanding requirements. North American alone got 40% of its revenue from space work. Any retraction on those contracts would weaken their share value.

On September 20, 1963 Kennedy made his historic offer at the UN in which he prepared his audience by declaring that there was a "pause in the Cold War", that conditions had changed and, referring to the Cuba crisis, asserted that Americans and Russians should "go to the Moon together" rather than "representatives of a single nation, but representatives of all our countries." Many saw it as a betrayal of trust while *Missiles and Rockets* believed it was "ill conceived", seeing the volte face as "dwindling from one of the most

BELOW: Key to developing new management techniques and a robust and more effective way of completing critical milestones, General Samuel C Phillips brought to NASA more than 100 senior US Air Force officers to effect major changes on the road to the Moon. (NASA)

BELOW: A model of the hypersonic X-15 rocket-powered research aircraft which was sent to the White House as a mark of JFK's contribution to the development of new air and space capabilities. (JFK Library)

exciting challenges ever accepted by a nation to an unimportant pawn in the Cold War to be sacrificed in the first gambit of appeasement." Kennedy acquired as many enemies the day he offered the Soviets a helping hand to put the hammer and sickle on the Moon than he collected at any other time.

Having received what he wrongly interpreted as a positive sign from Khrushchev, Kennedy moved rapidly to negotiate and then cement a potential agreement. Bundy worked with Schlesinger to draft a directive through the National Security Council. The word from the White House encouraged active discussion with Webb at NASA who was asked to gather support inside the agency, not all of whom agreed with this policy change. Four days later it was signed by Kennedy as National Security Action Memorandum 271 with a meeting at the White House scheduled for December 15 to discuss progress toward formal discussions with Moscow.

On November 16, 1963 Kennedy toured Cape Canaveral on his third and last visit during which he visited the launch complex where the fifth Saturn I was ready to begin placing payloads in orbit, fulfilment of the commitment made to equal Soviet capabilities in booster power. He was later flown to the USS *Observation Island* to watch the test firing of a Polaris missile from the submerged submarine USS *Andrew Jackson*, the first launch he had seen from Cape Canaveral. Just six days after leaving the Cape, Kennedy was assassinated.

Endless words have been written about his legacy and much has been made of his role in advancing the pace of the space programme, in funding the largest increase in funding NASA will probably ever see and in placing Americans on the Moon by the end of the decade. But a recording of his discussion with Webb on September 18, 1963 will probably stand as the most succinct and definitive account of how he himself saw the greatest technological endeavour of that century:

"I talked the other day…and said that I thought the space programme, looking ahead, unless the Russians did something dramatic and we don't have anything dramatic coming up for the next 12 months, so it's going to be an attack on the budget, but this looks like a hell of a lot of dough to go to the Moon when you can go – you can learn most of that you want scientifically through instruments and putting a man on the Moon really is a stunt and it isn't worth that many billions.

"Therefore, the heat's going to be on unless we can say this has got some military justification and not just prestige…Why should we spend that kind of dough to put a man on the Moon…we've got to wrap around this in this country, a military use for what we're doing… If we don't it does look like a stunt and too much money…the only way we can defend ourselves is if we put a national security rather than a prestige label on this…I mean, if the Russians do some tremendous feat, then it would stimulate interest again, but right now space has lost a lot of its glamour."

ABOVE: Denied the opportunity to see his Moon landing goal realised, models of the planned facilities at Cape Canaveral had been shown to the President during a visit on September 11, 1962. (NASA)

CHAPTER SIX

THE ARMS RACE

Throughout the 1960 election campaign Kennedy had merged the structure of defence, foreign policy, and peace mechanisms into a central thrust for a new America and a different world in which freedom and prosperity for a global community of nations was foremost on his agenda. For Kennedy, articulate and highly literate, the lectern from which he addressed his audience supported a robust and intellectual attack on incumbent Republican policies.

The launch of Sputnik 1 in October 1957 provided Kennedy with material to attack the Eisenhower administration and on November 7 that year the *New York Times* reported his response: "The people of America are no longer willing to be lulled by paternalistic reassurances, spoon-fed science fiction predictions, or by pious platitudes of faith and hope." Widening the frame of reference, the concept of a new America framed a major speech in February 1958 in which Kennedy targeted Soviet achievements in science and technology.

Using the Sputnik launches as indicative of a complacent country facing a communist propaganda coup again, Kennedy asserted that "the future is very dark indeed." In what many regard as a seminal speech on the state of the national threat, on August 14, 1958 he had argued before the Senate that "In the years 1960-64 the deterrent ratio (will) in all likelihood be weighted very heavily against us." In addition, he wanted to "reverse complacency" without expressing panic and "fix a course for the future that would restore American superiority."

Revisiting these concerns, in a speech in Wisconsin during November 1959 Kennedy argued that "we have fallen behind the Soviet Union in the development and production of ballistic missiles – both intercontinental and those of intermediate range," and in referring to the later stages of the Eisenhower administration, he sought to reverse "the years that the locusts have eaten." On January 23, 1960 he asserted that the US was "second in missiles," and on February 29 said: "it is indisputable that we are today deficient in several areas," and that "our deficiency is likely to take on critical dimensions in the near future."

Throughout 1960 Kennedy returned again and again to issues that he believed threatened the safety of the nation and repeatedly called for increased spending on missile procurement. On August 26 he addressed a convention for the Veterans of Foreign Wars and repeated those concerns. At the end of September, he declared that "The next President must promptly send to Congress a special message requesting the funds and authorisation necessary to give us nuclear retaliation power second to none." In a letter to the trade magazine *Missiles and Rockets* dated October 10, 1960 he proclaimed he would accelerate "our Polaris, Minuteman and other strategic missile programmes."

On accepting the nomination of the Democratic Party for President, Kennedy issued a stark declaration that should he win the election he would place strategic nuclear weapons high on his agenda. The party had

> "Throughout 1960 Kennedy returned again and again to issues that he believed threatened the safety of the nation and repeatedly called for increased spending on missile procurement."

BELOW: An atomic bomb test on Bikini Atoll in 1946 provided evidence for the measured effects from the blast, heat pulse, and subsequent radiation. Such direct measurements had not been possible at surface level with the bombs dropped on Hiroshima and Nagasaki. (Department of Energy)

WAR OF THE WORLDS

ABOVE: The development of thermonuclear, or hydrogen bombs in the 1950s produced substantially greater explosive yield and opened the way to the concept of 'massive retaliation' as a deterrent. (US Atomic Energy Authority)

With a disadvantage in strategic air power, ballistic missiles were a sure way of avoiding threats from enemy air defences. Russia had a long history of rocket research and during the 1950s developed a massive rocket, an Intercontinental Ballistic Missile (ICBM), identified in the West as the R-7 but designated by NATO as the SS-6 Sapwood, capable of sending atomic warheads from launch sites in Russia to targets in the United States.

In parallel, under Eisenhower and utilising breakthrough technology in larger rocket engines and smaller thermonuclear warheads, the Atlas ICBM was being developed in the United States. Neither SS-6 nor Atlas would be ready for test until the late 1950s while existing missiles such as Redstone, Jupiter and Thor had short or intermediate range and did not have the capability to strike targets at intercontinental distance.

'MISSILE GAP'

The ability for the Russians to strike North America with rockets panicked Americans unfamiliar with threats from the skies, let alone from ballistic missiles against which there was no defence. It created a concern that ran deep into the political campaigns of both the Republicans and the Democrats and as described in chapter five, these fears of Soviet capabilities detracted from the expected campaign issues around jobs, wages, and the economy. For the first time, Americans felt vulnerable to attack and with

already proclaimed that it would "recast our military capability in order to provide forces and weapons of a diversity, balance and mobility sufficient in quantity and quality to deter both limited and general aggressions."

It went further, calling for "Deterrent military power such that the Soviet and Chinese leaders will have no doubt that an attack on the United States would surely be followed by their own destruction." In such words were enshrined the pledge of the North Atlantic Treaty Organisation (NATO), established in April 1949 as a collective defence against Soviet attack facing what would become the Warsaw Pact of communist-led nations in May 1955.

Believing that the next war would be settled solely on the basis of air power, blunt force had been the mainstay of US Air Force doctrine. The army and the navy subscribed to the concept of "balanced force." The air force had the confidence of the majority of Americans and politicians and followed that - strong air power implied safety at home; fighters would defend the skies while bombers would obliterate the enemy.

The doctrine of massive retaliation had been formally declared by Secretary of State John Foster Dulles on January 12, 1954, the year after the armistice signed with North Korea paused a conflict that had threatened to escalate into atomic warfare. Combining security with solvency, the Eisenhower administration had threatened all-out nuclear war with Russia while relying on smaller ground forces in Western Europe, backed up with a large range of tactical nuclear weapons in NATO countries.

The world in which Kennedy sought high political stature was immersed in the dual doctrinal principles of national security and defence while the rhetoric by outside sources assumed high levels of authority and debate over alternative policies. For NATO countries, the United States was the pact leader both in spending and in the production of conventional and nuclear weapons. Seeking ways to pose an equivalent threat to the United States as that presented by encirclement, Russia wanted a means of threatening the United States with the same scale of atomic conflict it perceived to be the threat from the Western alliance.

ABOVE: President Kennedy and his Secretary of Defense Robert McNamara were convinced that a change in the way nuclear weapons were considered for use in time of war was essential. (NARA)

CHAPTER SIX

> "On accepting the nomination of the Democratic Party for President, Kennedy issued a stark declaration that should he win the election he would place strategic nuclear weapons high on his agenda."

ABOVE: In the event of war, new jet-powered bombers introduced by the US with the B-52 (top) would be used against targets in the Soviet Union shared with the British Vulcan as part of a Single Integrated Operation Plan (SIOP). (USAF)

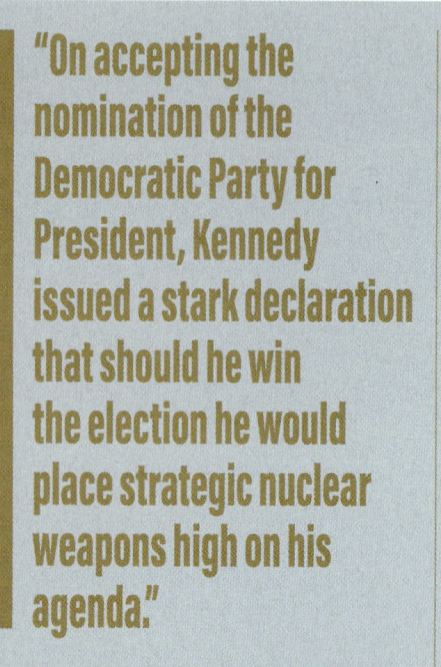

some justification imagined that they could be destroyed in their homes by missiles launched from the Soviet Union.

The exact state of Soviet missile capabilities, force levels and effectiveness were unknown to the intelligence services, the Pentagon and the wider public, let alone the politicians who sought to use these fears for partisan causes. Even the separate armed services got in on the act, using these concerns to bolster bids for more funding, greater force capability and expanded resources. It would be known as the 'missile gap' but there was precedent for such dangerous and unqualified assertions.

Only a few years previously, scare stories about an acceleration in Russian bomber production fuelled by patriotic and hawkish advocates of enhanced military air power had been unleashed by the trade press. In its February 15, 1954 issue, *Aviation Week* revealed new photographs of the latest Russian bombers for what it described as the new Soviet 'Sunday Punch'. The following week it published comments from former defence secretary Stuart Symington that "we may now be looking down the barrel of a possible intercontinental attack," concluding with a warning questioning whether the Soviet Union now had "the weapons necessary to accomplish its oft-announced intention to destroy the free world."

The bombers were types incapable of reaching North America or prototypes under test which did not precede full production as envisaged by Western observers. During the annual air display at Tushino, in July 1955 the Russians flew 10 prototype bombers over the viewing stands, adding eight more before returning and giving the impression of a larger formation. Based on flawed predictions of Soviet factories capable of producing airframes, Western observers interpreted this to imply that 800 would be operational within five years.

These extrapolations, based on observed propaganda from inflated Soviet deception at Tushino, estimated that the maximum potential production output at Russian bomber factories to be five times that later acknowledged by the intelligence community to be a realistic expectation. But the myth prevailed long enough to influence increased US bomber production funded by panicking politicians voting for higher budgets. It also stimulated support for the Lockheed U-2, which had been personally endorsed by Eisenhower seeking better intelligence concerning the Russian arms industry and its resource and production capacity.

The reality saw around 140 operational strategic bombers with Russia's frontline aviation units in 1960, never getting above 170 throughout the remaining 30 years of the Soviet Union. By far the majority were turboprop-powered Tupolev Tu-95, or Tu-142 variants for the Russian navy operated from land bases. In 1960, the US Air Force had 1,735 bombers in the

ABOVE: The Soviet threat of nuclear attack on North America rested solely with their long-range bomber, the Tupolev Tu-95 with the NATO code name *Bear*. Slow and noisy, it was not a seriously credible threat. (USAF)

inventory capable of striking targets in the Soviet Union. During the late 1950s Russia placed higher priority on the production of ballistic missiles on land and in submarines for threatening the United States and for nuclear deterrence and it was this that created the 'missile-gap myth' to supersede the myth over the number of Russian bombers just a few years earlier.

TRUTH TO POWER

Kennedy's understanding of the state of national defence is far from straightforward and is in two distinctly separate channels. First, schooled within an establishment that believed the Soviet Union to be a threat to national survival, both main political parties in the US unequivocally supported a numerically and qualitatively superior defence force. Anything less was anathema to the average voter, which explains the public and partisan outrage that there could be superior quantities of Soviet bombers capable of reaching the United States.

In a broader context, Kennedy was unsure about the concept of massive retaliation enshrined by Eisenhower, and this is important to an understanding as to why the new President would seek to encourage a more nuanced posture. Yet ever the savvy politician he knew that it would be electoral suicide to question that doctrine before achieving office. This would bring difficult choices. The information to which he was responding as a candidate for the highest office was very different to that which he was briefed on in the months up to his election.

Secondly, there was continuing debate over Soviet missile numbers and here again a myth emerged that the Russians were out-building the US. It was an impression defined through public fears aroused by the launch of Sputnik and the visible demonstration of a rocket that could launch nuclear warheads across intercontinental distances. In fact, development of the US Atlas ICBM was not so far behind that of Russia's SS-6, the Soviet missile making its first successful flight on May 15, 1957, with Atlas on December 17.

ABOVE: A firm advocate of a pre-emptive strike against the Soviet Union, General Curtis LeMay had masterminded the firestorm raids on Japan during World War Two and worried the Kennedy administration that there was a need to constrain decisions over who could authorise the use of nuclear weapons. (USAF)

Conflating the unknown estimates of Soviet missile production with the published facts of the US ICBM programme, in 1959 critics of the Eisenhower administration published estimates from public sources in several US newspapers and magazines. It was from these that Kennedy got figures that polarised his focus. On January 12, 1959, the *New York Times* published an appraisal by Richard Witkin stating as fact that in 1960 the Soviets would have 100 ICBMs to America's 30 and that by 1964 the imbalance would grow to 2,000 versus 130. In its February 9, 1959 issue *Aviation Week* went further, claiming that the Russians already had 100 ICBMs, growing to 600 by 1962.

Secretary of Defense McElroy was at pains to point out that the National Intelligence Estimate (NIE) projected a superiority in US ICBM production and that the Russians would not achieve parity in either capability or production quotas. This led to some calming of the hyperbole and resulted in a slightly modified projection by journalists, *Fortune* magazine claiming in its April 1959 edition that the Russians currently had 10 ICBMs but that this would grow to 500 by 1961.

Kennedy maintained his rhetoric in what was a defining period for criticising the Eisenhower administration. Information

ABOVE: In an attempt to calm fears about Russian threats of nuclear attack, the US government circulated booklets and advice describing how to achieve some protection, but few were convinced about the plausibility of such measures. (DoD)

CHAPTER SIX

BELOW: The Boeing B-52 posed a formidable threat to the Soviet Union and production plans were based on a false interpretation of just how large the Russian bomber force was, revealed subsequently to be much smaller than expected by the 'missile gap myth'. (USAF)

was certainly available on a need-to-know basis, from the U-2 spy plane overflights of denied territory to signals intelligence obtained from a wide range of platforms including land sites in Iran and Turkey. A Top Secret CIA report dated July 17, 1960 drew stark conclusions, that "many of our guesses on important subjects can be seriously wrong, that the estimates which form the basis for national policy can be projections from wrong guesses and that, as a consequence, our policy can indeed be bankrupt."

Despite concerns from Eisenhower that overflights might result in a U-2 being shot down, a flight was allowed to go ahead from Peshawar, Pakistan, to Bodø, Norway on May 1, 1960. It was shot down near Sverdlovsk and its pilot, Gary Powers captured. The flight path had taken it over Baikonur, Kazakhstan, and the Plesetsk rocket launch sites near Archangelsk not far from the White Sea where ballistic missiles were being tested.

For Eisenhower this was a seminal moment to reset the agenda, constrain further U-2 overflights and deepen his commitment to get the true facts out to the public. That included involving the competing contenders for the presidential election later that year in the hope of levelling the true state of affairs between the military capabilities of the US and the Soviet Union. Perhaps surprisingly, active voices in the missile-gap controversy grew less vocal as the year progressed.

THE MYTH REVEALED

Although opportunities to deploy the U-2 were drastically reduced, the top secret spy satellite programme known internally as

ABOVE: The high-ranking Russian spy Oleg Penkovsky provided information to a British agent about the inadequacies of the Soviet missile forces, their slow development and the very low numbers deployed. (The Spy Museum)

Corona and operated under the public name Discoverer was in full-scale development. Flight trials began in early 1959 and on August 19, 1960 the first full capsule of film showing Soviet military installations was recovered from Discoverer 14 and sent for analysis. This mission returned more information than had been obtained by all preceding U-2 flights combined. As a result, the NIE estimate that there could be upwards of 140 Soviet ICBMs in service during 1961 was downgraded to between 10 and 25, a figure which itself is now known to have been far too high.

Highly attuned to the potential damage from escalating myths and political mischief, Eisenhower called Vice President Nixon and explicitly directed him to reveal the real situation regarding Soviet missile developments to the candidates for Presidential election. Although a Republican, Eisenhower wanted the Democratic nominee fully appraised of the facts. Kennedy had been selected to stand for President at the Democratic National Convention on July 13, 1960 and the decision to include him in the highest level of intelligence was unusual, although not unique.

Ten days after the nomination, Kennedy was given a briefing lasting almost three hours by the CIA's Allen Dulles at his home in Hyannis Port. Lyndon Johnson, the nominee for vice president, received his briefing on July 29. Kennedy

50 JFK – A LIFE REMEMBERED

BELOW: Represented here by an early Mk 1, to achieve an overwhelming ability to respond to a Soviet first-strike the US Air Force introduced the Minuteman missile based in underground silos for some protection against attack. (USAF)

consistently complained that he was not given information allowing him to make an independent assessment of the true situation and that he was denied details from the U-2 flights. However, diaries verify that he was given extensive access to military bases and provided with targeted briefings.

In late August he visited the headquarters of Strategic Air Command (SAC) at Omaha, Nebraska and was given a day-long tour by US Air Force officers and provided with details at the behest of the Eisenhower administration. Believing that he had not been given the detail he wanted, he would complain that he had received more information when he was a member of the Senate Foreign Relations Committee. Records of both this and the Armed Services Committee of which he was a member show that he rarely attended.

The late congressman Charles S Gubser recalled that the information to these committees showed "CIA, air force, army and composite intelligence estimates of each Russian capability" which revealed that the "missile gap did not exist," adding that "1960 was a busy year for Senator Kennedy. He may not have found time to attend." Neither had Kennedy attended any of the highly detailed and classified sessions provided from May 27 to June 2 in which a five and a half hour presentation by Dulles "included elaborate maps, charts and U-2 photographs" deemed so secret that the stenotyped tapes were destroyed.

Kennedy received a further CIA briefing on September 19, one month after Discoverer 14, indicating that estimates on Soviet missile deployments were grossly exaggerated and that US production was likely far greater than in Russia. There is indication of a third visit and in his biography of McNamara, historian Henry Trewhitt reveals that a navy intelligence captain flew to Hyannis Port, Massachusetts to caution John Kennedy "that the national intelligence estimates did not support the frightening calculations of Soviet strength. Kennedy would not accept the figures," adding that "He was after all, a politician just short of the greatest prize the nation could offer."

Kennedy persisted in quoting figures for which there was available evidence to the contrary and stuck with the mass trend and went along with the missile-gap myth. Yet for all his compliance with trends, Kennedy had well defined, if complex views on the possession and expansion of nuclear weapons and platforms for their delivery. When running for the Senate back in 1956, he endorsed a statement from his friend Clinton Anderson who declared that "I think the United States should take the leadership in bringing these tests to an end." Kennedy added: "And I think we owe it…because we are the only country that engaged in atomic warfare in the last war."

ABOVE: In 1962, the Kennedy administration introduced the 'Duck and Cover' plan for educating children about the ways they were to act if a nuclear war began. It included rehearsals in schools and meeting places which brought mixed reaction! (NARA)

CHAPTER SIX

ABOVE: The Cheyenne Mountain Complex in Colorado, from where a major nuclear war would have been commanded, was designed to protect staff and equipment against attack, with special communications to prevent a loss of contact at critical times along the command chain. (USAF)

There is no way of knowing precisely what Kennedy did know about the relative positions of US and Soviet missile numbers but there is abundant evidence to show that he was aware of the top secret estimates that fell far short of those he repeated during the election campaign. At the very least Kennedy exaggerated the figures available regarding missile numbers and on reaching office was quick to reverse that position and use information from satellite photographs to reassure the American public that their worst fears were unjustified.

Perhaps of greater implication was the impact this had on the election. During October 1960 Kennedy began to import missile-gap fears into his campaign at a significantly higher level and the polls showed a marked increase in support for him as a result. It is hard to state that this was decisive on the election result, but there was a concerted effort on the part of campaign managers to brief the press on the 'great debate' involving the claimed overall unpreparedness of American security.

SHIFTING POLICIES

The President is the civilian commander-in-chief of all US military forces and Kennedy brought in as his Secretary of Defense (SecDef) Robert S McNamara, a man from industry with a high-performance record and an impressive history organising large-scale strategic ventures – during war and in peace. Skilled in spreadsheet management and recruited from his position as president of the Ford Motor Company, McNamara would introduce novel, innovative concepts such as 'flexible response' and the dark arts of systems-management, techniques essential to the demands of an increasingly complex arms industry.

The Kennedy administration inherited a new way of organising and integrating different strategic nuclear forces under the Single Integrated Operational Plan (SIOP), which had been introduced on August 16, 1960. The US Air Force had been seeking such a plan for eight years and its adoption required close coordination. When Kennedy and McNamara were sworn in one overriding concern was the state of the nation's missile programme at a time when the gulf between public awareness and certain knowledge was arguably the widest it had ever been since the bomber-gap myth of the mid-1950s. Promises made by Kennedy to enhance the US national defence posture excited the senior air force leadership.

Eisenhower had already set the US on a road to nuclear superiority with a triad concept of land, sea, and air delivery systems for nuclear warheads. These were very different to the warheads first deployed by Strategic Air Command – now smaller, more accurate and with options for deployment on ballistic missiles, in protective silos on land or in submerged submarines at sea, or by an all-jet bomber force in the US or at numerous allied bases around the globe.

The triad concept guaranteed that no single operating or design flaw with any one system could neutralise the deterrent. While the early Atlas rockets were incapable of rapid response due to their non-storable propellants, later missiles such as the Titan II and the solid propellant Minuteman could be kept at a state of immediate readiness. This ensured that there was time to fire a retaliatory response even after the Soviets had launched a pre-emptive attack.

With election campaign promises for a stronger and bigger strike force, the air force was eager to advise the incoming administration as to its needs for a much more robust and enveloping attack posture. Based on Kennedy's pre-election promises of an expansion in defence spending, in May and June 1961 the US Air Force drew up plans for McNamara, quoting a need for 3,190 ICBMs of which 2,500 were silo-based, 415 were mobile Minuteman missiles and 275 Titan II. Kennedy was averse to this on two grounds: the general escalation in strategic nuclear missiles concerned him for the reciprocal consequences from a Soviet response and the mobile missiles were a potential breakout from the concept of deterrence.

Kennedy was worried that the United States was still living in the age of 'massive retaliation' and that this skewed judgement when it came to the consequences for

ABOVE: The US government spent considerable resources on the plan for protecting its citizens from injury in a nuclear attack, very little of which was convincing. (NARA)

> "The ability for the Russians to strike North America with rockets panicked Americans unfamiliar with threats from the skies, let alone from ballistic missiles against which there was no defence."

excessive firepower. Kennedy refused to accept that the country with the most weapons of this kind could fight and be the sole survivor in a nuclear war. This was a great leap of faith, where nuclear weapons became the instrument of insurance against global war.

A key factor in air force requests for higher ICBM and bomber force numbers was the perceived threat from this missile gap. For a year after the inauguration, it was still a contentious issue, but the quoted numbers were now a fraction of former predictions. A classified intelligence estimate presented to the Senate Armed Services Committee on January 19, 1962 claimed the Soviets had "about 25 ICBMs" but even that was grossly overestimated.

Kennedy and McNamara sought to move US defence policy to a more nuanced and flexible strategy, adaptable and responsive to various levels of hostility from brush-fires to all-out nuclear war. In support of that politically motivated *realpolitik*, Kennedy refashioned the US military so that it had the equipment and the strategies to engage conventional forces in a wider range of conflicts than would have been possible under the old order where nuclear weapons were the only means of response.

Kennedy himself was horrified to learn that, had communist forces taken the Korean peninsula, there had been a clear and decisive plan to use atomic weapons during the 1950-1953 conflict. Even to the point of attacking China to prevent it reinforcing communist forces from North Korea. During the Eisenhower years conventional force levels had been allowed to run down, leaving little option other than to 'go nuclear' in the event of a major confrontation.

Both Kennedy and McNamara were shocked to learn through briefings immediately before they were sworn in to office, of just what was planned. The exact way SIOP would be implemented is classified to this day, but the first completed attack plan designated SIOP-62 was flexible only in the mode selected. There were separate optional and coordinated attacks for a pre-emptive strike, which would be authorised on the basis that it was believed the Soviet Union was about to strike, or in reaction to a strike on the United States from the Soviet Union.

In a pre-emptive strike, 3,200 nuclear weapons would have been unleashed on Russia, China, and East European countries of the Warsaw Pact. These would have dropped 7,847MT on 1,060 targets not only in Russia but simultaneously in China. It was always assumed that it would be a war against the communist bloc, irrespective of who posed the perceived threat. Of that total about 40MT was allocated to Moscow, an explosive yield on that target alone almost two thousand times the yield of the atom bombs dropped on Hiroshima and Nagasaki combined. In responding to a direct attack on the US, the SIOP-62 plan envisaged delivery of 1,706 nuclear weapons on 725 targets in the same areas as those for a pre-emptive strike and including 130 cities.

Confronting the dilemma created by the proliferation of nuclear weapons, Kennedy made the restoration of Presidential control of their use a priority. The widespread distribution of such weapons on a variety of different delivery systems, in locations at home and on allied bases around the world greatly increased the possibility of accidental use or theft. It was vital to ensure that they could never be used without verification from the White House. Of greatest concern was the Permissive Action Link (PAL) consisting of a locking device on each weapon that could only be released through a valid combination releasing the trigger mechanism.

Most weapons had a four-digit code, but many had a 12-number code. In either case, only a few attempts were permitted before the trigger self-destructed rendering the weapon inoperable. Other precautions against tampering would have the same effect. There was also a mismatch between

ABOVE: Obtaining information about Soviet war plans and on the amount of air and missile systems they had deployed had prompted spy flights with the Lockheed U-2. This flight path was the one planned for Col Gary Powers, on which he was shot down and subsequently placed on trial. (Author's collection)

CHAPTER SIX

> "Only a few years previously, scare stories about an acceleration in Russian bomber production fuelled by patriotic and hawkish advocates of enhanced military air power had been unleashed by the trade press."

ABOVE: The President meets with the Joint Chiefs of Staff, one in a series of summits that began to transform the way the Department of Defense would wage war, shifting from 'massive retaliation' to a policy of 'flexible response'. (NARA)

weapons which required Presidential sanction to provide the codes and others, from the earlier day of deployment, which provided local commanders with those same authentication codes. Kennedy worked closely with McNamara to ensure that additional safeguards were put in place.

Despite protests from the US Air Force, the size of America's strategic nuclear arsenal was stabilised by actions taken during the Kennedy administration and would eventually result in deployment of 1,000 Minuteman and 54 Titan II ICBMs, all in fixed silos, and 656 Polaris missiles in 41 nuclear-powered submarines, a total of 1,710 missiles capable of striking the Soviet Union and China. Kennedy was taken with the idea of moving the nuclear deterrent from land-based silos to hidden locations in the world's oceans so as to minimise the attractiveness of encouraging the enemy to target populated areas preserving the deterrent intact.

The larger concern for Kennedy was the proliferation of tactical and strategic nuclear weapons of all types delivered by land, sea, and air. In 1947 the US had 23 atom bombs and by the start of the Korean War in 1950 it had 198. By the time Kennedy came to office in 1961 there were 18,638 nuclear weapons in the US inventory in numerous locations across the world. The Russians had approximately 1,600, none of which could reach the continental United States. By the end of that year the US had 22,229, the Russians about 2,400.

Policies introduced by the Kennedy administration and the checks and balances put in place to constrain a runaway escalation appears in retrospect to have in fact been a licence to build. By 1962 the US nuclear stockpile had increased to 25,540 and to 28,133 in 1963, peaking at 31,255 by 1967. For many, the supremacy of US military power was an inherent need in a turbulent world and the monopolar position held by the US nuclear deterrent was deemed by them to be essential.

REDEFINING WAR

Almost immediately after taking office and in a display of long-term intentions, Kennedy ordered a position paper titled *A Review of North Atlantic Problems for the Future*. Compiled by Dean Acheson, the report was approved by the President on April 21, 1961 and transmitted to the National Security Council as a document titled *NATO and the Atlantic Nations*. Its wording defined the rationales behind Kennedy's decision to downgrade the incremental steps precipitating nuclear war.

It proposed expansion of conventional forces in Europe capable of holding the line against any Soviet incursion into Western Europe.

The function of nuclear weapons in the European theatre was to be primarily diplomatic, their use to be only as an

ABOVE: With fictitious markings and declared to be conducting weather research, the U-2 provided vital information where it could but insubstantial for any realistic assessment of Soviet capabilities. (USAF)

ABOVE: Some decisions made by McNamara were flawed, as with the General Dynamics F-111 which was developed in the mistaken belief that the requirements of the US Air Force and the US Navy could be met by a single aircraft design, the Navy's F-111B shown here being cancelled. (USN)

additional and rather minor contribution to general nuclear war. In a seismic shift in policy, it expressly forbad local commanders from using nuclear weapons, even in self-defence, without the explicit authorisation of the President.

The ensuing debate escalated to a bitter contest between those in the field wanting many more nuclear weapons, greater dispersal, and free use as seen fit and those within the administration seeking to cut back on nuclear weapons. The official report asserted that "the demise of the massive-retaliation policy was imminent if not actual. The doctrine of flexible response had arrived even though it had yet to be implemented."

Some in the administration had wanted the dispersal plan to be abolished completely, but that was not to be, a moderated plan being adopted instead. It touched a sensitive nerve, many US field commanders disliking the dispersal of nuclear weapons to allies in Europe where there was dual control. Under a bilateral agreement the UK was first to accept full and unquestionable deployment of as many nuclear weapons on their territory as the US said it required, for both operational use and as a deterrent.

That model had been applied to other countries. The US provided the warheads for nationally owned delivery systems, be they aircraft, tanks, artillery shells, torpedoes, or mines, under a two-key procedure whereby American technicians installed the warheads. One US officer and one from the host country would have to insert separate keys simultaneously at two separate control panels on site.

Because the host nation could elect not to insert the key, opponents of this concept asserted that the command to launch thus "hung by the thin thread of one key." The operating concept was thus rendered divisive in that both had to agree on one position, which meant removing total control from the US chain of command.

Nevertheless, the concept of flexible response was a cornerstone of the Kennedy administration and fixatedly applied by McNamara. In a gathering of world leaders at the UN on September 25, 1961, the President went beyond the acknowledged constraints of political expediency by connecting his long-term views on defence and deterrence with the fate of civilisation:

"Today, every inhabitant of the planet must contemplate the day when this planet may no longer be habitable. Every man, woman and child lives under a nuclear sword of Damocles, hanging by the slenderest of threads, capable of being cut at any moment by accident or miscalculation or by madness. The weapons of war must be abolished before they abolish us… The events of the next ten months may well decide the fate of man for the next ten thousand years… Together we shall save our planet or together we shall perish in its flames."

The policy reshaped by McNamara on Kennedy's insistence and well debated during the electoral campaign totally changed the way conventional and nuclear strategy was written. An outlier to the military European consensus, considerable input to flexible response came from the British. Chief of the defence staff, Lord Louis Mountbatten told McNamara that "under no circumstances, even with the great superiority in nuclear weapons that NATO had…should we consider" their use.

The fundamental changes brought about by the 'New Look' defence policy mobilised in 1961 by the Kennedy-McNamara doctrine were based on three tenets: the ability to fight two major conflicts and to contain a regional brushfire at the same time; a phased use of nuclear weapons such that an aggressor would face unacceptable 'assured destruction' in retribution for a first strike; and a no-cities policy.

The no-cities policy was made possible by the significant increase in targeting accuracy, already held by the manned penetrating bombers, and by the enhanced accuracy of the ICBM and SLBM forces. Kennedy wanted to see the deterrent shift from counter-value (cities and urban) to counter-force (military) targets. Anticipating that all three legs of the triad would soon be capable of striking Soviet land-based silos and bomber bases, McNamara went to work to implement a strategy which would change for ever the face of defence planning in all NATO countries.

ABOVE: The development of smaller and less powerful nuclear weapons shifted reliance from massive bombs capable of destroying entire cities to bombs capable of providing a scaled response proportionate to the threat, as with the Mk 28 shown here. (National Museum of the USAF)

CHAPTER SEVEN

BERLIN

Two potentially catastrophic encounters would each take the world to the brink of all-out nuclear conflict and demonstrate the futility of micro-planning a violent confrontation with weapons of immense destruction. The first involved a Cold War standoff between NATO and the Soviet Union, a tension that began in Europe two years before the Presidential election. The second would involve a close encounter with the continental United States and missiles in Cuba.

It started during Kennedy's first tour of European countries, with a visit to France on May 31, 1961 and a speech delivered at the Elysée Palace. It was delivered in the presence of Charles de Gaulle, the tall, elegant statesman who had held France's future in waiting during the dark years of Nazi oppression, leader of the Free French and who led the government from November 1945.

A joint statement issued on June 2, the eve of Kennedy's departure confirmed "their commitment and responsibilities toward Berlin." The former capital of a once proud country, Berlin was a symbol of deteriorating relations between the US and the Soviet Union. The focus for this European tour was to meet Premier Khrushchev in Vienna. Austria had been granted neutrality by the victorious powers in 1945, while Berlin, deep inside East Germany and 145km (90 miles) from the West German border, was a divided city separated into zones run by Russia, the US, France, and Britain.

ABOVE: The division of West Berlin into sectors controlled by the British, French, and Americans faced Soviet troops across the eastern sector and around the periphery of the allied nations with East Germany. The three permissible air corridors are shown.
(Leerlaufprozess)

56 JFK – A LIFE REMEMBERED

To enormous fanfare, before an exquisitely choreographed reception committee watched by 1,500 newsmen, Kennedy arrived at Vienna's Schwechat Airport on the morning of Saturday June 3, 1961. At 12.45pm from the steps of the ambassador's residence, the President received Premier Khrushchev, who emerged from his black Russian limousine especially delivered from Moscow. Initial discussions would last almost six hours around a lunch of Beef Wellington.

This meeting had been anticipated for some time. Initial contact between the two powers had been made when Khrushchev sent Kennedy a congratulatory message on the day he was elected. It expressed a desire to put US-Soviet relations back to the place they were during the Roosevelt Presidency, when much trust had been placed in discussions with Stalin about the post-war world.

Khrushchev claimed that he wanted to meet to discuss ways to achieve disarmament, to present "A German peace treaty and other questions which could

ABOVE: Pivotal to events that would unfold as pressure was brought to evict allied forces from West Berlin was the formation of the Warsaw Pact forces in 1955. It combined military manpower from former East European states and half a divided Germany. (Author's collection)

ABOVE: Douglas C-47 transport aircraft rotating at Tempelhof Airport, Berlin during the blockade of 1948-1949 when the Russians cut access for all forms of transport except by air. (USAF)

bring about an easing and improvement of the entire international situation." Kennedy reciprocated in kind and continued to support such goals, sending Khrushchev a letter on February 22, 1961 seeking a meeting for an "informal exchange of views."

Attitudes hardened after the failed Bay of Pigs fiasco where CIA agents and Cuban exiles had mounted a surprise attack on April 17, 1961 with the aim of ousting pro-communist Fidel Castro. This debacle soured relations and advisers close to Kennedy reminded him that the Soviet premier was a master at embarrassing his opponents, at using any opportunity to gain advantage.

So soon into the Kennedy administration, several State Department officials cautioned the President that he could easily fall foul of a public showdown.

The US ambassador to Moscow also advised against a meeting but Robert Kennedy supported his brother and preparations had gone ahead. So it was with a degree of trepidation from staff and expectation that Kennedy began his first face-to-face meeting with Khrushchev. Not without the assistance of intermediaries, however. Many times, throughout the Kennedy administration spies, double-agents and interlocuters were used to convey messages back and forth between the White House and the Kremlin.

A key figure in that was Georgi Bolshakov, single-handedly responsible for playing intermediary between parties during the 1961 Berlin Crisis and in setting up the Vienna Summit. Recruited by Robert Kennedy, Bolshakov was a GRU (Soviet military intelligence) officer, that most engaged of Soviet operative organisations. GRU was adept at working in the shadows and recruiting Western operatives in turn. With a press pass to the White House, Bolshakov was well placed to manage all those aspects in addition to his official cover.

Robert Kennedy first met Bolshakov in 1954, the second time during the evening on May 9, 1961 when his press officer, Ed Guthman arranged the connection which took place on the steps of the Justice Department in Washington, DC. Leaving Guthman behind, the two men walked along the Mall and sat down to discuss how the GRU man could draw the President and Khrushchev together at a neutral location. Without having to engage with the Russian ambassador to Moscow, Mikhail Menshikov for whom there was little respect at the White House.

As they sat and talked, lightning shattered the evening, a storm broke out and the two men ran back to Bobby Kennedy's office with soaking wet shirts which they removed to dry out. Sitting down in their undervests while thunderclaps broke and lightning seared the sky, they began to discuss precisely how the two most powerful men in the world could be brought together over deeply divisive issues. Nobody else was there and contact between the two, arranged openly under the guise of an informal chat to a journalist, was kept confidential.

Approved of by the President, it allowed a back channel to open, circumventing officials at the Pentagon and the State

CHAPTER SEVEN

Department of whom, after the Bay of Pigs, the two brothers were increasingly suspicious. For his part, Khrushchev could leak through Bolshakov precisely what he wanted Kennedy to believe and even before it began that June day in Vienna, the Soviet Premier was already calling the shots.

FROM CONVERSATION TO CRISIS

The main issue on the agenda for Vienna was Berlin. The Soviet Premier sought to assuage fears from Walter Ulbricht's GDR party that East Germany was being slowly depopulated and would Moscow please close the Berlin border? There was truth in the fear, more than 2.7m East German citizens having moved to the West since 1945. Khrushchev worried that the West could intervene and further destabilise East Germany and wanted to conduct a separate peace treaty with Berlin which would require the withdrawal of US, French, and British forces.

That first day had been as much about each learning the body language and the posturing style of the other than it was about serious negotiation. Over the late lunch both men discussed a range of issues, a verbal dance teasing out attitudes, strengths, and weaknesses.

During the after-lunch toast, Kennedy was curt and brief, hoping for further and more productive discussions, while Khrushchev droned on about how together the two countries could control the world and stop any other nuclear power from starting a war with drastic consequences. Driving a wedge between Kennedy and the 'hawks' in his administration, Khrushchev declared that the U-2 spy flights were clandestine attempts to increase US-Soviet tensions.

After their lunch the two men strolled in the ambassador's garden, Kennedy walking a straight line while Khrushchev hovered and bobbed around, observers noting the dissimilarities between the two; the rotund and portly Khrushchev shorter than the youthful Kennedy, his shoulders slightly hunched but otherwise slim and very slightly tanned. It seemed to irk the Soviet Premier that the leader of the free world should have 23 years on him and so little experience of government.

Returning inside and speaking privately with only interpreters in attendance, Kennedy uttered the seminal admission to Khrushchev that he had made a mistake over the Bay of Pigs. In return he received a lecture on how a handful of Castro's followers had overturned the 'oppressive' Batista regime in 1953 with Khruschev adding that "Castro is not a communist, but US policy can make him one." Khrushchev had Kennedy on the back foot, extracting an admission from the President that he had not been a fan of Batista, adding with a chillingly prescient judgement that Cuba would never be a threat to the United States.

Failing to mention Soviet interventions in East Germany in 1953 and Hungary in 1956, Kennedy lost ground as Khrushchev bristled at suggestions that Poland may seek to align itself with the West. The day ended with a level of mutual acrimony and a tense withdrawal into entrenched positions. The general conclusions from those present believed that Kennedy had demonstrated profound inexperience when confronted by the wily Khrushchev.

That night, both men had dinner with the Austrian president but Kennedy was sidetracked when Khrushchev repeatedly tried to open for discussion issues that could not be solved over a single meeting. It again drifted into tension when Khrushchev emphasised that he was determined to offer a separate peace treaty to the GDR. As Khrushchev departed, Kennedy turned to Ambassador Thompson and asked rhetorically "Is it always like this?" The response was predictable: "Par for the course!"

MOPPING UP

Day two of the Vienna mini-summit began with the ball in Khrushchev's court. "The man is inexperienced, even immature," he told his interpreter Oleg Troyanovsky, snapping that "compared to him, Eisenhower is a man of intelligence and vision." Some of the problems Kennedy would encounter this day were the result of having conducted detailed planning through Bolshakov, with his brother's predilection for secret negotiations unknown to the White House staff and key officials.

Some of Kennedy's inner circle were ill-suited to the President's needs, most urging him to take control of the talks, to maintain a rigid line following the agreed agenda.

ABOVE: Children and youth workers unloading pallets from a C-74 Globemaster that had brought supplies in during the blockade of Berlin (USAF)

ABOVE: President Kennedy with De Gaulle in Paris before he travels to Vienna for the summit over Berlin. (NARA)

BELOW: The Russian Embassy in Vienna where Kennedy met Khrushchev on the second day of the talks dates back to the Tsarist days and retains all the splendour of that age. (Stadler/Bewag)

Sensing this inflexibility due to a lack of experience, Khrushchev again had the edge over Kennedy, catching him off guard by straying into areas on which the President had not been previously briefed. Failed by his advisers, Kennedy was wrong-footed from the start of talks on June 4.

This time the President was hosted by Khrushchev at the Soviet embassy, where he arrived promptly at 10:15am. Built in 1872, the building was uncharacteristically imperial for a Soviet stronghold because the palatial edifice had been acquired for the Tsar in 1891, complete with trimmings. Prior to the meeting, the Kennedys had attended Sunday Mass at St Stephen's Cathedral where Jacqueline had been visibly moved as she knelt in prayer. The crowd of spectators at the Russian embassy was dwarfed by the throng that had gathered earlier at St Stephens in this very religious capital.

At their morning discussions Khrushchev emphasised the Soviet view of the Berlin issue as one embedded in deeper concerns about German hegemony in two world wars. There was a belief, he said, that it would remain a threat to European peace and order, pledging never to let go its control of the GDR, inferring that occupation of liberated East European countries would ensure a greater level of stability. Khrushchev reminded Kennedy that with West Germany in NATO, Russia considered it a future threat.

Kennedy responded by reminding Khrushchev that occupation of sectors in Berlin had been agreed by the Allied powers including Russia and was not a negotiable matter with the GDR, as it would have to be if East Germany signed a separate peace treaty with Moscow. Khrushchev hardened his line, asserting his non-negotiable intention to sign such a treaty and to evict non-Russian allies from Berlin. But the Soviet Premier confirmed that they accepted American influence over the future of West Germany, implying that the US should view that as a concession on their part and nothing else.

Kennedy held his ground, perhaps more assertive and assured than on the previous day, reminding Khrushchev that "West Europe is vital to our national security and we have supported it in two wars. If we were to leave West Berlin, Europe would be abandoned as well. So, when we are talking about West Berlin we are also talking about West Europe," adding that the US would never give up territory gained through "rights of war." With Khrushchev getting visibly angry, Kennedy pushed home the core message by reminding him that the US and its allies "are in Berlin and have been there for 15 years. We suggest that we stay there."

ABOVE: Kennedy went face-to-face with Khrushchev and found an arrogant and intractable adversary wielding a big stick and threatening to eject the Americans from West Berlin. (NARA)

ABOVE: In reality a thorn in Khrushchev's side, East Germany's Walter Ulbricht pressed for a peace treaty with Russia and a level of independence which he hoped would ensure renewal and industrial growth. (Author's collection)

CHAPTER SEVEN

BELOW: The architectural elegance of St Stephens cathedral as it appeared in 1847 according to artist Jakob Alt, the place where Jack and Jackie Kennedy went for mass during their stay in Vienna. (Jakob Alt)

While the morning meeting ran its course, the leading wives were on a tour of Vienna. Over lunch the two leaders discussed a suggestion Kennedy had raised on the previous day that the Soviet Union might like to consider joining America in sending men to the Moon. Kennedy had declared that objective to a joint session of Congress only 10 days previously and this is the earliest known date at which he raised that as a possibility. As noted previously, it would became a major initiative two years later.

The day ended with a delayed departure by Kennedy as he insisted that he would try one more time to get a satisfactory answer from Khrushchev on which they could mutually build a solution over the proposed peace treaty with East Germany. Kennedy had an instinctive political belief that his charm, charisma and youthful enthusiasm for solutions could trump compromise but Khrushchev would have none of it. Seeing a hint of frustration, the Soviet leader drove home his determination to secure a separate treaty with East Germany, declaring that "force will be met by force. The US should prepare for that, and the Soviet Union will do the same."

ABOVE: Relaxing and reading at his home, Konrad Adenauer had mixed relations with the US government, serving as the first post-war Chancellor of West Germany from 1949 to 1963. A man of significance, however as tensions mounted between the two halves of this divided nation. (Bundesarchiv)

Kennedy flew to London on June 5 to meet Prime Minister Harold Macmillan, leader of the Conservative Party and Prime Minister from January 1957 when he had replaced Sir Anthony Eden. Kennedy had received a drubbing from Khrushchev and the President's entourage noticed a profound change in his demeanour. For the first time it seemed he realised that there was an intractable issue facing an insoluble dilemma over the Soviet commitment to a peace settlement that could bring US and Russian troops together at gunpoint.

Departing for London, turning to Kenneth O'Donnell, his special consultant and appointments secretary, Kennedy remarked that "All wars start from stupidity…it seems particularly stupid to risk killing a million Americans over an argument about access rights on an autobahn in the Soviet zone of Germany… If I'm going to threaten Russia with a nuclear war, it will have to be for much bigger and more important reasons than that." On which matter Kennedy was concerned that if it did come to that it should be started as a decision by the President and not "by a trigger-happy sergeant on a truck convoy at a checkpoint in East Germany."

It was supposed to have been a charm offensive against the grey-suited men from the Kremlin, an opportunity to dazzle the Soviets. But 1960s Russians didn't respond well to demonstrations of glitz and glamour, offensive to hard-liners schooled in dark tactics, crafted on subterfuge, honed through conspiracies, and obsessed with ideological struggles. It was a missed opportunity that could have been reversed had a better understanding of the Russian mind set prevailed. But that would be an error perpetuated by several Western governments down the decades as they tried to get their way with intractable Russian leaders.

When Kennedy touched down in London, Macmillan saved him from the rigours of a formal meeting and hosted the President at private quarters in Admiralty House. Kennedy was in no physical condition to follow a formal and very public display of cordiality. Instead, it was sandwiches washed down with whiskey during a deep discussion that began at 10:30am and went on far longer than the two hours assigned. After which there was a meeting with Foreign Secretary Douglas-Home with the three men crafting a speech for Kennedy to give on arriving back in Washington DC.

In painful agony from his ailing back injury and full of medication to defer incapacity, on the way back home across the Atlantic Kennedy sat on the floor of

ABOVE: Georgi Bolshakov was a Soviet agent and political go-between, fetching and carrying messages between Robert Kennedy and Khrushchev over the type of discussions the Kremlin wanted, access being granted by his press pass. (Author's collection)

Air Force One in shorts surrounded by aides and advisers, ruminating over the bleak resistance to any form of compromise from Khrushchev. Given the company and uncharacteristically quiet, his inner circle was visibly depressed over the outcome. There was very little joy to be had from the visit to Vienna, lingering as it did on the margins of humiliation.

Kennedy sought rest and as he dismissed the group he asked his secretary Evelyn Lincoln to file away classified documents. A piece of paper slipped out from one of the folders, on which he had written the words "I know there is a God – and I see a storm coming; If He has a place for me, I believe I am ready." It was an extract from the words of Abraham Lincoln in 1860 referring to the challenge of abolishing slavery. Evelyn thought it was a foreboding of death; it was in fact Jack Kennedy's portent of a very great challenge looming ever closer.

When they got back to the White House the Kennedys were in low spirits. Alone with his brother in the White House, Jack Kennedy was nursing pain – both physical and mental as he went over the two days in Vienna again and again. As noted later by Bobby, watching as tears ran down Jack's face, he recalled that he had "never seen my brother cry before about something like this."

Together reflecting on the mini-summit, Jack turned to his brother and, almost as if tormented by acknowledgement of the inevitable, declared that "If nuclear exchange comes, it doesn't matter about us. We've had a good life, we're adults. We bring these things on ourselves. The thought, though, of women and children perishing in a nuclear exchange. I can't adjust to that."

Not explicitly evident at the time, this was in effect a cathartic moment for Jack and Bobby Kennedy. A coming of age in a troubled, turbulent, sometimes violent and always shocking world of international intrigue, subterfuge and mind games. It was as though he had completed a rite of passage and come through the first challenge of his Presidency – facing down a leader who played by different rules. From this day Jack

ABOVE: The West Wing of the White House and the Rose Garden on which Jackie Kennedy spent considerable attention to its redesign. Many walks were taken here to discuss deals with the Russians. (NARA)

CHAPTER SEVEN

> "To enormous fanfare, before an exquisitely choreographed reception committee watched by 1,500 newsmen, Kennedy arrived at Vienna's Schwechat Airport on the morning of Saturday June 3, 1961."

Kennedy was the commander-in-chief that the nation looked on him to be.

Some, notably Dean Acheson had wanted preparations for all-out war while others urged caution. Pentagon adviser Paul Nitze set up a special task force to get a position paper ready for McNamara to review and forward to Kennedy about the precise sequence of actions needed.

THE GATHERING STORM

Despite reservations, Kennedy was faced with stark warnings over the possibility of doing too little, too late. Acheson believed that Berlin was only a problem because Khrushchev had made it one and that his confidence only rested on the belief that "the United States and its allies will not do what is necessary to stop him," that the only way out was to show them that "what they want to do is not possible."

Irreconcilably it seemed, two camps were forming. The Hard Liners on Berlin (HLBs) of Acheson, Nitze, Lyndon Johnson and the German desk at the Department of State, and the Soft Liners on Berlin (SLOBs) represented by Schlesinger, consultant Henry Kissinger, Bunday, McNamara and Soviet affairs adviser Charles Bohlen. The SLOBs were closer to Kennedy and probably represented the most immediately influential group.

While the United States and Soviet Union squared off for a major confrontation, planning for a major lockdown of East Germany under the ruling communist GDR party was in an advanced stage of preparation. But there was disagreement over the practicality of isolating East Germany from West Germany, considered the only solution to the mass emigration. But the movement of 250,000 people across the Berlin sectors by train, car and foot every working day would bring almost insoluble challenges.

The obvious solution was to build a wall across the line dividing the Soviet sector from those for the other three allied powers, while simultaneously placing a barrier between East and West Germany. The sectors had been only roughly drawn up in 1945 without the precision necessary for a defined barrier to be laid out on the ground. Khrushchev called for more accurate maps, which had to be redrawn to a surveyor's standard for practical construction.

The situation for East Germany was dire. The working-age population was bleeding away and most of those leaving the country were more highly educated. Recognising the opportunities across the border in free Europe, many had already risked all to escape the oppressive and economically depressed system. The division between the Berlin sectors were the easiest crossing points. The national border with West Germany had been hard-wired to prevent illegal crossings, the optimum place to depart.

Showcased in the West, former East German resident Marlene Schmidt had escaped her native country in 1960 and won the Miss Germany contest held in Baden-Baden. Fellow citizens, housed in Ulbricht's bland and depressing urban monstrosities, jury-rigged aerials to pull in TV signals showing the lissom beauty compete with other girls. Flying to Miami, Florida, Marlene walked away with the Miss Universe competition, drawing a furious riposte from Ulbricht.

The *Junge Welt* (Young World) magazine branded her a "display piece" with nothing more going for her than "bust, butt and hips," the government-run propaganda machine pledging to prevent any more of East German's youth from escaping to a similar fate, declaring that "the world will forget you." It did not. In 1962 she married the actor Ty Hardin and had a daughter, becoming an actress, movie producer and screenwriter before she returned to Germany and a life in Saarbrucken where she lives now.

Ulbricht claimed he had been the architect of the wall plan but Khrushchev had pulled his puppet's strings despite the East German leader pleading for permission to do so since 1952. As planned, the wall would follow a snaking line extending a build-length of 156km (97miles) covering 43km (27miles) with sharp turn points to divide streets, apartment blocks and open spaces. Eventually the permanent wall would be a double structure with an average height of 4m (13ft).

Between the two parallel walls human guards would patrol the space with orders to shoot deserters on sight, mines creating a 'death strip' and trained killer-dogs on line-runners to snatch down any would-be escapees. Work would take some time to complete but in the meantime, a large force of soldiers and workers would set up barriers and guard posts so as to trap as many people as

ABOVE: Present in the shadows while discussions went ahead between Kennedy and Khrushchev, Warsaw Pact chief of military staff Aleksei Antonov helped organise plans for military action. (Author's collection)

ABOVE: Kennedy chats with Willy Brandt, the mayor of West Berlin from 1957 to 1966, but who had numerous disagreements with Konrad Adenauer, and at times with Kennedy himself. (Marion S Trisosko)

possible. It was planned that bulldozers would start tearing up roads to stop traffic moving between the zones and notice would be served requiring people to remain off the streets.

Meanwhile, at the White House the hawks and the doves were each seeking the approval of the President for their respective positions. Acheson's initial report came under scrutiny from a small team led by Schlesinger who cautioned the President not to repeat the mistakes of Cuba by placing "excessive concentrations on military and operational considerations" rather than the politics and consequent ramifications.

Schlesinger advised the President not to present an ultimatum to Moscow. A stark message delivered to show strength of will would probably not help and Schlesinger explained the danger that this could invoke. For him it was a test that "becomes an end in itself rather than a means to a political end" and that the looming crisis had "nothing to do with Berlin, Germany or Europe (but) a fateful test of wills."

Schlesinger's advice was for Kissinger to head planning for the US response. Khrushchev had himself repeatedly quoted the date of December 31. There was still a lot of work to be done and Kissinger seized the opportunity to place himself centre-stage by putting to Kennedy a policy document encapsulating the situation with realistic options for the United States.

"The fate of Berlin is the touchstone for the future of the North Atlantic Community," he said, cautioning the President that an unsatisfactory response could demonstrate "the West's impotence." For Kissinger, it was a purely political issue and that "the West simply cannot afford a defeat in Berlin," by which he meant a loss of face in a highly staged showdown with the global audience.

A gathering of senior advisers at Kennedy's Hyannis Port home on July 8 afforded the opportunity to vent some of those opposing views. It had not been a good start to the day. Moscow was seven hours ahead of Massachusetts' time when news arrived that this day Khrushchev had announced to rapturous applause that he was rescinding a previously announced plan to cut the Soviet army by 1.2million men while increasing his defence budget by one-third. Tensions were rising.

ABOVE: Soviet tanks move up to Checkpoint Charlie as tensions rise over access to the East Berlin sector by bona fide diplomats and western embassy staff. (NARA)

RIPOSTE AND RESPONSE

On his speedboat *Marlin*, Kennedy scolded Rusk for not yet having provided a response paper to the unexpected memo handed to him at Vienna. Only later was its fate untangled. The response had indeed been sent to the White House as Kennedy requested and on time but his office had misplaced it. A replacement was duly delivered. Unfortunately, it was locked away for security and the only holder of the combination away on a two week vacation and nobody knew it was there. Not a good start.

Two critical meetings of the National Security Council (NSC) provided opportunity for Kennedy to hear the evidence and decide on which path to follow: Acheson's hard-line approach or Schlesinger's incremental, step-by-step counter as events moved, an all-out threat to massive retaliation or a series of graduated stages so as not to provoke Moscow into perilous actions.

The first meeting of the NSC on July 13 saw Rusk soften the Acheson approach to the frustration of Lyndon Johnson who supported a more robust line. Bundy summarised four possible approaches: An immediate reinforcement of US forces; a harder line introducing all forms of preparedness short of declaring a national emergency; issuing that but short of calling up reserves; no significant military build-up but with an emphasis on it as a political challenge rather than a military one.

The second NSC meeting six days later appeared to confirm a phased approach, McNamara not wanting a large reserve force mobilised without a specific mission. Kennedy made it clear that while he was still undecided on the specific sequence, a more nuanced approach was definitely favoured. Kennedy crafted a speech to the American public, televised nationwide beginning at 10pm Eastern time on July 25. Lasting a long 31 minutes, this was a very different President.

The speech was a cathartic moment for the American public and Kennedy knew that much more hinged on his words that evening than anything he had said before. During that afternoon he had taken to a long, soothing bath in only partial attempts to dull the pain from his aching back. His public were bruised too, by the embarrassment of a national humiliation over the Bay of Pigs, the Moon dash goal delivered exactly two months before in response to yet another Soviet success a mere wisp in the wind to what was now required of the world's most powerful leader.

After the hot bath and characteristically sitting alone eating his dinner on a tray, Kennedy went over his speech again and again, recognising an inadequate ending, calling Evelyn Lincoln to dictate down the telephone a major amendment drawn from an overarching view of the global tension. 'Exchange'? Jack hated that word. Strike it for 'annihilation'. By his own admission, the very thought of ordering down upon ordinary people death and destruction on such a colossal scale terrified him. Which was probably just as well.

ABOVE: Marlene Schmidt served a propaganda coup on the East German government when she fled her communist masters and became Miss World, attracting degrading remarks about her from Walter Ulbricht. (Dean Johnson)

CHAPTER SEVEN

ABOVE: US Army tanks barrel-to-barrel with Russian tanks at the crossing between the sectors. (NARA)

Arriving at the Oval Office at 9:30pm on July 25, 1961, Kennedy met the technicians who would transmit his speech over radio and television. To control the sound quality, the air conditioning had been switched off and the room began to get uncomfortably warm, perspiration breaking out on Kennedy's forehead as he waited while the networks called in and verified transmission links. In the compact Oval Office where it was highly unusual to stage a national broadcast, 60 people and seven TV cameras added heat to the still hot and humid evening in Washington DC where temperatures that day had reached an uncomfortable 34°C (94°F).

He began with a summary of the situation in West Germany and in West Berlin, explaining the reasons why the US, Britain, and France were there and why it was essential to remain, asserting that it might be necessary to use force to do so. Kennedy then shifted to summarise steps already taken by his administration to strengthen US defence forces and the nuclear deterrent. In a specific example cited he affirmed that 50% of the bomber force had been put under an alert status which would allow them to become airborne within 15 minutes.

Turning to what may be necessary in the future, Kennedy described how he was to request supplementary defence funds from Congress for raising US Army manpower from 875,000 to a million men with increases of 29,000 for the navy and 63,000 for the air force. Draft calls were to be tripled and reserve levels increased. Ship and aircraft marked for retirement would be retained with additional money for conventional weapons and stocks. For civil defence, Kennedy announced that he would increase the number of facilities available to the general public for shelter which would be identified and stocked with food, water, medical supplies and essential equipment.

Overall, it was evident that Kennedy had not accepted Acheson's hard-line approach, that he would not declare a national emergency but rather a scaling effect to progressively respond to Soviet initiatives and that he was asking Congress for approval to make significant increases to the defence budget. This was a 'new' Kennedy, one for whom statesmanship and statecraft went hand-in-hand with the potent capabilities in the defence forces at his command and the policy decisions pending.

A week after the televised address to the nation, Kennedy debated the consequences of his decisions with White House adviser Walt Rostow. Walking with Rostow in the Rose Garden, Kennedy debated the levels to which Khrushchev would descend to keep the countries of Eastern Europe intact. "If East Germany goes, so will Poland and all of Eastern Europe," said Kennedy, "he will have to do something to stop the flow of refugees. Perhaps a wall. And we won't be able to prevent it. I can hold the Alliance together to defend West Berlin, but I cannot act to keep East Berlin open."

GATHERING CLOUDS

On August 1, 1961, Ulbricht was driven to Moscow in a blacked-out limousine of the kind that saw fast travel up the centre lane of the main roads in the country's capital reserved exclusively for the privileged elite and state officials. He was there to meet Khrushchev for a detailed planning session lasting 2hr 15min on how to seal off East Germany from the rest of Berlin. Agreement was crucial before the Soviet Premier took it to the other Warsaw Pact countries for a briefing on plans which was to be held August 3-5. No information about this leaked through agents to the West, the White House being completely unaware of the hastened schedule.

Ulbricht learned that Moscow was about to deploy an additional 4,000 troops to East Berlin and that additional tanks would be positioned along the border with West

ABOVE: The standoff at Checkpoint Charlie only gradually dissipated when Khrushchev decided that it was not worth a war, telling Ulbricht that he would not be signing a peace treaty which would have inflamed tensions and probably resulted in conflict. (NARA)

Germany. Khrushchev was unwilling to shut access routes by land or air, recognising that the NATO countries would not settle for that and do what they had 13 years before when Stalin had attempted to isolate Berlin. Khrushchev asked Ulbricht when he would be ready for the wall. "Do it when you want," came the reply, "We can do it any time."

Counterintuitively considering the political control Russia had over its Warsaw Pact neighbours, East European countries were becoming increasingly reliant on trade with the West. From the outset, dissent was clear, Poland insisting that East Germany pay compensation should trade deals collapse because of this action. Hungary's János Kádár protested that a third of Hungary's economy depended on trade with the West of which a quarter was with West Germany alone.

Ulbricht had set the position clear in his conversation with Khrushchev on August 1, here translated from the declassified transcript: "For two months there have been no potatoes to buy in the GDR. The reason is that we had a very bad harvest last year and this year the weather was humid, with the result that the potatoes spoiled on the clamps. Otherwise, the use of butter is increasing in the GDR, and we don't have enough butter.

"The planned deliveries of milk were not fulfilled in half of the districts in the GDR. We had to order that butter be given out with potato ration cards since we still have potato ration cards. All of this produced a hostile mood among the people. This is seen for example in the events in Hennigsdorf. With this we can see that the use of butter hasn't decreased, but instead has remained at the previous level. We only just introduced rationing. In addition, we have forbidden the making of cream out of milk, which is also not liked by many people. In this time of the year, for vegetables we usually have only sauerkraut and sour cucumbers on the market. But in this year, we never had even potatoes."

But the emigration figures too were shocking for economists; already 3.4m East Germans had left for the West since 1948, almost 20% of the population. East German citizens were fleeing the country in increasing numbers, 20,000 in June 1961 and 30,000 in July with departing aircraft at full capacity. The influx left West Germany strained to absorb the numbers and businesses and industry was saturated with former East German workers arriving with skills, good qualifications and high expectations.

Some reports from the CIA gave Kennedy heart that there was a way through, but there was no indication at all about the pace at which events would move and no sign that plans were at an advanced stage, blueprints having already being drawn up by Bruno Wansierski who had been placed in charge of the massive construction project by Ulbricht's security chief, Erich Honecker.

On August 4 the foreign ministers of the US, the UK, France, and West Germany began a three-day meeting in Paris to

> "Sitting down in their undervests while thunderclaps broke and lightning seared the sky, they began to discuss precisely how the two most powerful men in the world could be brought together over deeply divisive issues."

BELOW: The Clayallee where, not without some provocation, US Army units stridently tried to press across into East Berlin. (Peter Kuley)

CHAPTER SEVEN

BELOW: Unknown at the time, several nuclear delivery systems had been armed and put on alert, including the Davy Crockett 'rifle', capable of discharging a very small nuclear warhead. (US Army)

discuss the situation and debate options. Nobody wanted military action but the West Germans spoke for economic sanctions on East European countries. They also sought an increase in the deployment of nuclear weapons in Europe. The KGB had been monitoring the secret meetings and conveyed the gist of the talks back to Khrushchev.

At this point there was no awareness in the West that the barbed wire and machine-gun posts would be set up within days or that eventually these would be replaced with a dual-wall of concrete construction. On August 6 the 513th Military Intelligence Group received word from a secret agent that Ulbricht would totally close off the Eastern sector and set up a permanent barrier. Three days later it received verification that foot traffic would be stopped and that a more complete isolation of East Berlin was pending.

The sealing of East Berlin from the rest of the city began on the evening of Saturday August 12, long before anybody in the White House had anticipated closure. Signals intelligence indicated a flurry of activity that appeared to precede a major event but the analyses were inconclusive and several advisers suggested that these may be efforts to defer suspicion. There was some comfort when news arrived that Khrushchev was heading for a break on the Crimea.

A profound state of uncertainty and nervousness prevailed. But notwithstanding that, the Kennedy family had the afternoon off aboard their boat *Marlin* in Nantucket Sound for a relaxing few hours swimming and enjoying the hot sunshine.

THE CONCRETE ROSE

By the early hours of Sunday August 13, trucks had rolled onto the streets of Berlin where the wall would be defined by concrete bollards and barbed wire barriers. Troops quickly set up machine-gun posts denying access to non-uniformed personnel. S-bahn (city) and U-bahn (underground) trains were banned from travelling into or out of East Germany, tracks were torn up and shutters placed on windows facing into the allied sectors.

Before sunrise the city had been ringed with troops and security officials and there was no opportunity to move between the sectors. Three Soviet divisions had moved close to Berlin and Ulbricht ensured the border with West Germany was patrolled in depth.

The first news to get out of Berlin to the West clattered onto the Reuter's News teleprinter at 1:11am where British journalist Adam Kellet-Long began to read a 10,000-word statement from Moscow. Full of recriminations against the West and explaining what was already underway, it also reassured NATO countries that access to Berlin would remain open. Once again, the stick and the carrot.

Galvanised into action, Kellet-Long dashed to his car and sped off down the dark, empty streets to see what was going on. Turning into the Unter den Linden he was stopped by a policeman and turned back. Returning to his office he sent his first report: "Earlier today, I became the first person to drive an East Berlin car though the police cordons where the border controls began shortly after midnight."

Across the British, French and American sectors, East German troops dashed to the border with the West to secure the frontier into East Germany, turning around to point their guns on their own people to prevent them crossing into the West. It was as bizarre as it was chilling, frequent announcements on East German radio declaring the new restrictions on movement interspersed with American jazz tunes. Again, the stick and the carrot; we have constrained you but you are free to live your lives.

Now commanding US military forces in West Berlin, Gen Albert Watson II sent a helicopter up to observe events unfolding where protests had already broken out

> **"It seemed to irk the Soviet Premier that the leader of the free world should have 23 years on him and so little experience of government."**

ABOVE: Over time, in 1961 the Russians and the East Berlin soldiers and police put up a concrete barrier in the form of a double-wall where 140 people would die trying to escape from East Berlin and find a way to the West, while 229 people out of 5,000 attempts were successful. (Thierry Noir)

against the temporary and hastily erected barriers defining the line where a double concrete wall would soon be erected. Explosions were heard across the city as police and East German troops fired teargas at the angry crowds. What Ulbricht called his 'concrete rose' had fully flowered.

It was approaching 1pm on Sunday when Kennedy's military aide Brig Gen Chester V Clifton radioed the motorboat *Marlin* informing them that "I've got a top priority message from Washington. You must turn the President around and come back to shore." The message from the situation room at the White House was succinct, informing the President that events had moved quickly and that East Germany had locked off its sector of Berlin and closed access to the British, French and American sectors to all but legitimate autobahn and air transport. Kennedy was visibly annoyed, asking "How come we didn't know anything about this?"

A report from Ulbricht to Khrushchev on July 15 urged the Soviet Premier to move quickly to prepare and sign a peace treaty with East Germany. In his response, Khrushchev was reluctant to push the West further, noting that "since the measures for the securing and control of the borders of the GDR with West Berlin were carried out successfully, and since the Western powers are tending towards negotiations…such steps which could exacerbate the situation should be avoided. It is especially appropriate to abstain from new measures which would change the control order set up by the GDR government on the border with West Berlin."

Two days later at the 22nd Congress of the Communist Party of the Soviet Union, 4,413 delegates heard Khrushchev announce that it was no longer necessary to complete a peace treaty with East Germany by the end of 1961. The Chinese were critical of the Russians for having presented a response which appeared to weaken them with respect to the Kennedy administration, leaving open the accusation that the initial strong tone was merely a bluff which would only serve to encourage 'the enemy'.

BELOW: On June 26, 1963, Kennedy delivered a rousing speech of encouragement to the people of Germany's divided city, declaring "Ich Bin Ein Berliner" ("I am a Berliner") but he would not live to see the wall torn down by the hands of thousands in June 1990. (Author's collection)

SUBSCRIBE

FlyPast

FREE GIFT WORTH £30.95!

FlyPast is internationally regarded as the magazine for aviation history and heritage.

shop.keypublishing.com/fpsubs

Britain at War

FREE GIFT WORTH £35.95!

Britain at War is dedicated to exploring every aspect of the involvement of Britain and her Commonwealth in conflicts from the turn of the 20th century through to the present day.

shop.keypublishing.com/bawsubs

ORDER DIRECT FROM OUR SHOP...
shop.keypublish

OR CALL +44 (0)1780 480404

(Lines open 9.00-5.30, Monday-Friday GMT)

TODAY

SAVE UP TO £30 WHEN YOU SUBSCRIBE!

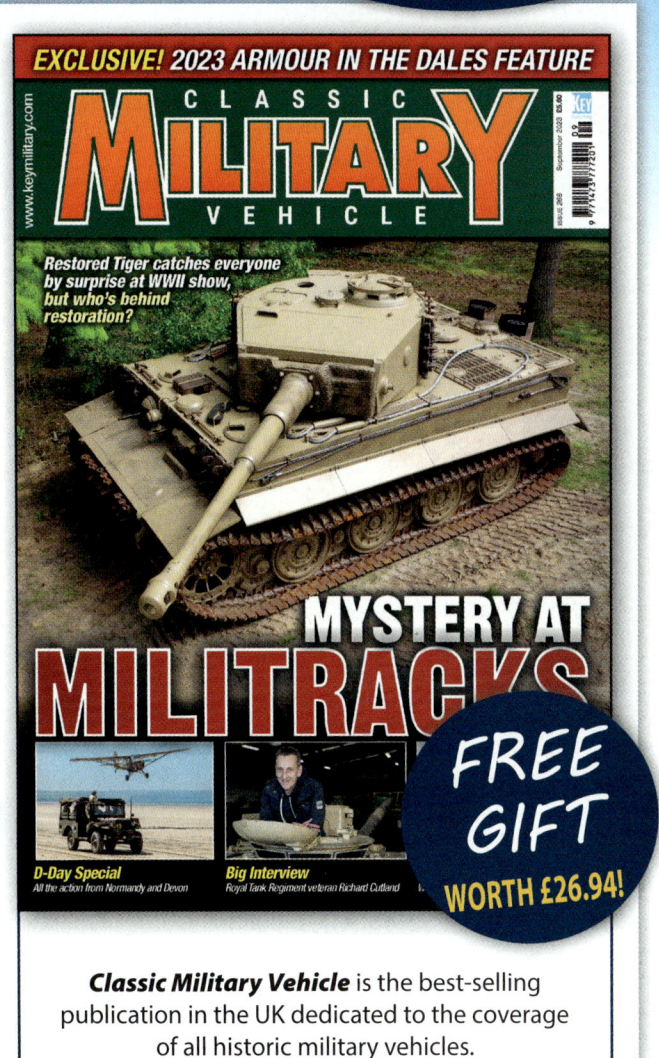

FREE! SPITFIRE SURVIVORS SUPPLEMENT

Aeroplane
HISTORY IN THE AIR SINCE 1911

SPITFIRE SALUTE

Celebrating 80 years of MH434... and your guide to the world's air...

FREE GIFT WORTH £28.94!

Aeroplane is still providing the best aviation coverage around. With focus on iconic military aircraft from the 1930s to the 1960s.

shop.keypublishing.com/amsubs

EXCLUSIVE! 2023 ARMOUR IN THE DALES FEATURE

Classic Military Vehicle

Restored Tiger catches everyone by surprise at WWII show, but who's behind restoration?

MYSTERY AT MILITRACKS

D-Day Special – All the action from Normandy and Devon
Big Interview – Royal Tank Regiment veteran Richard Cutland

FREE GIFT WORTH £26.94!

Classic Military Vehicle is the best-selling publication in the UK dedicated to the coverage of all historic military vehicles.

shop.keypublishing.com/cmvsubs

CHAPTER EIGHT

CUBAN CRISIS

Unbeknown to Kennedy at the time, the Berlin crisis had played a crucial role in defining the threats his administration would encounter over the next two years. First, in challenging America's image abroad as the technological superpower of the century after Sputnik and Gagarin, then in trapping the US into vast expenditure on a massive arms race accelerated by the 'missile-gap myth', and then by challenging the Allied presence in Berlin.

Now schooled in the nuances of the diplomatic response to crises, Kennedy held his nerve over the Berlin lockdown and waited for further moves from Khrushchev, which never really came in the way expected. On August 18 Kennedy sent 1,500 soldiers along the autobahn from West Germany to West Berlin to demonstrate that in the event the Soviet Premier reneged on his commitment not to change the routes of access he would use military force to keep it open.

The note from Khrushchev to Ulbricht explaining that those 'old' assertions were no longer relevant had been publicly distributed to send the Kennedy administration reassurance that Moscow was not prepared to go to any war that would involve the Warsaw Pact facing down NATO forces. Kennedy was openly relieved, and as a few advisers had said after the Vienna mini-summit, Khrushchev was testing the will of the new President and the solidity of the Western alliance.

Kennedy understood that the wall did nothing for the people of East Berlin and that the border with Western Europe, now consolidated across a stronger ring of barbed wire, checkpoints, and machine gun towers, was an admission of failure. It was a denial of hope for East Germans as a whole. But Khrushchev thought entirely the opposite, declaring that he had won and that "the United States and its Western Allies had no choice but to swallow a bitter pill as we began to take certain unilateral steps."

Steps which included a massive display of Soviet military power to which Western observers were invited for the first time since 1936 and intended to drive the message home and obtain maximum propaganda

ABOVE: Taking his responsibilities to the limit, General Lucius Clay insisted on patrolling the streets bordering East Berlin, persistent in his intent on challenging the Russians to the annoyance of the army leadership. (US Army)

ABOVE: Berlin became the trigger for the Cuban Missile Crisis as M-48 Patton tanks faced off Russian armour and confused troops at Checkpoint Charlie, uncertain about their next moves. (DoD)

70 JFK – A LIFE REMEMBERED

CUBA

> "Clay had conducted exercises in woods around the outskirts of West Berlin practicing how to use tanks as bulldozers to smash through Soviet-style defensive barriers."

ABOVE: Sent to calm the activities of General Clay, General Bruce C Clarke was head of US operations in West Germany. (US Army)

value in their claim that they had prevailed. In a sequence of increasingly robust statements, Moscow ramped up the pressure on the US at a time when Kennedy believed it was all over. The White House braced itself for increased hostility.

On Kennedy's handling of the Berlin crisis the West German ambassador to the US Wilhelm Grewe would later recall that he "got the feeling that sometimes he was not absolutely sure himself whether it was appropriate to preserve a completely passive attitude at the time or whether he should have tried a more active policy to prevent the erection of the wall."

For the Russians, however, the matter had not been fully resolved and Khrushchev was now about to try his hand applying further pressure on Kennedy. Bolshakov was again the messenger. When Kennedy and his entourage landed at New York's La Guardia airport in the evening of Sunday, September 24, 1961 Salinger received a message from Bolshakov urging that he meet with Mikhail Kharlamov, at this time the press director at the Soviet Foreign Ministry.

Kharlamov is an interesting player in the power balance between Khrushchev and Kennedy, having been the face of the Soviet Foreign Ministry throughout the events surrounding talks over Berlin. He was well known to the international press and to Pierre Salinger and Bolshakov spirited him into the Carlyle hotel, the stopover point for Kennedy's visits to New York, by the side entrance.

Kennedy had a lot of 'insider' people conveying messages and one such had been journalist Cyrus L Sulzberger, asked by Khrushchev to convey a confidential message to the President. Kharlamov wanted to know if Kennedy had read the note. Khrushchev had asked Kennedy if they could agree "informal contact…to find a means of settling the crisis without damaging the prestige of the United States." Kharlamov said Khrushchev was worried about troop increases in Western Europe.

Into the early morning hours of September 25, Salinger conferred with Kennedy who telephoned Dean Rusk to finalise a reply to Khrushchev. Kennedy was in New York to deliver a speech to the United Nations, which he did later that day. This speech was regarded as one of the finest he had ever made and solidified the impression that this was a very different man to the one which had been elected, one for whom the realities of a dangerous and turbulent world had been fully accepted.

But there were detractors and increasing concern over the seemingly belligerent approach by Lucius Clay, technically just an adviser to events in Berlin but a key figure in shaping events over the next several weeks. Two days after the UN speech, General Bruce Clarke, head of Allied operations in West Germany, was sent to Berlin to stop Clay conducting repeated patrols up and down the autobahns in what was being interpreted as a provocation.

He advised General Watson that the show of military force was not permitted and that US armed units could no longer be employed on such tactics. It didn't help that Clay had conducted exercises in woods around the outskirts of West Berlin practicing how to use tanks as bulldozers to smash through Soviet-style defensive barriers. None of this was ever reported to Kennedy.

Unknown to the Americans, Russian spies saw these exercises and Khrushchev believed that plans were being drawn up to attack East Germany. He responded through the note from Kharlamov by setting up a covert communication channel between himself and Kennedy as a means of pre-empting any misinterpreted moves that could precipitate war. It was one of the most guarded secrets of the Kennedy brothers, maintaining close contact far outside the usual channels.

ABOVE: During the Berlin crisis, the allied air forces of NATO were held at readiness and in the UK that comprised the V-bomber force, represented here by the Vulcan in anti-flash white. (RAF)

www.keymilitary.com 71

CHAPTER EIGHT

Known as the 'pen-pal letters', the exchanges began on September 30, 1961 and would continue for the next two years. On that day at around 3:30pm, Bolshakov delivered a 26-page manuscript from Khrushchev, asserting that "You and I, Mr President, are leaders of two nations that are on a collision course," and as if inviting reconciliation, added that "We have no choice but to put our heads together and find ways to live in peace."

Bolshakov and others secretly used 'letter boxes' (drop-points) to deliver notes and manuscripts to Salinger and several others who had the ear of the President. But the intent was far from conciliatory; Khrushchev was under fire from hard-line Kremlin types blaming him for being too soft on the Americans, for not demanding stiffer conditions over Berlin and for stalling stronger moves to challenge the US over its expanding strategic nuclear capabilities.

Khrushchev knew that he had to soften the tone, show better performance in order to preserve his own position and believed that he could turn the President on or off like a dial, tuning the response according to how he posed threats – or offered baubles. After the Vienna mini-summit, all through the tensions over East Germany, the entrenched positions of the two leaders over Berlin appeared to have calmed the 'hawks' and satisfied the 'doves', those who sought conciliation and co-existence.

Thus began a continuous exchange between the two leaders outside the usual diplomatic channels at the Department of State, an agency which Kennedy distrusted. A view which was and would be taken by past and future Presidents who believed that the bureaucratic fog of formal and protracted negotiations got in the way of simple solutions. Witness the famous 'walk in the woods' by US negotiator Paul Nitze and Soviet Ambassador Yuliy Kvitinsky when trying to work out arms control agreements in 1982.

Openly and in public, Khrushchev would continue his bluff and bluster but in clandestine messages, notes, and letters for the President alone, he was placid, mild, and appealed for balanced debate. The Soviet Premier was playing a very dangerous game, appearing as two different people to separate audiences. Khrushchev was still facing much criticism, many unable to forgive him for denouncing Stalin, over his lack of progress in converting third-world countries to communism, over his love of foreign trips, and his cult of personality over pragmatism.

However, both JFK and his brother Robert were happy with this covert arrangement – outsiders were never quite as highly trusted and there was always the suspicion that opponents were conspiring. For this reason, the Kennedys courted intermediaries reporting back on rumours, dissident opinions, on schemers and plotters and on those seeking to engage at a confidential level for their own aggrandisement.

But the administration was burdened by fast-moving events inherited from the Eisenhower years, not least the aftermath of the attempted Bay of Pigs invasion. These defined an increase in the threat level over the coming months, already pointing toward far wider publicised brinkmanship in the coming year. To a place not very far from the shores of the United States itself.

ABOVE: A senior member of the US Embassy staff and here in discussion with Jack Kennedy, Allan Lightner pressed the Russian authorities and made open journeys into East Berlin to challenge their right to close the crossing. (NARA)

THE CUBA OFFER

Largely unrecorded in almost all popular histories covering Kennedy's life in government, his administration was compromised by the siting of 30 Jupiter Intermediate Range Ballistic Missiles (IRBMs) in Italy and 10 in Turkey from 1961. With a range of 2,400km (1,500 miles) they could reach deep into Soviet territory and the Eisenhower administration had also approved 60 Thor IRBMs, deployed to the UK beginning in 1958.

Kennedy allowed the Jupiter deployments to go ahead but had misgivings about the potential for a reciprocal deployment of equivalent Russian missiles closer to North America. Moreover, outdated and of limited military value, there were many who said they should never have been deployed and that they served no useful purpose.

ABOVE: John McCone (right) when representing the US Atomic Energy Authority with (to his left) Paul Foster, US representative to the AEA, and Ambassador John Graham. (NARA)

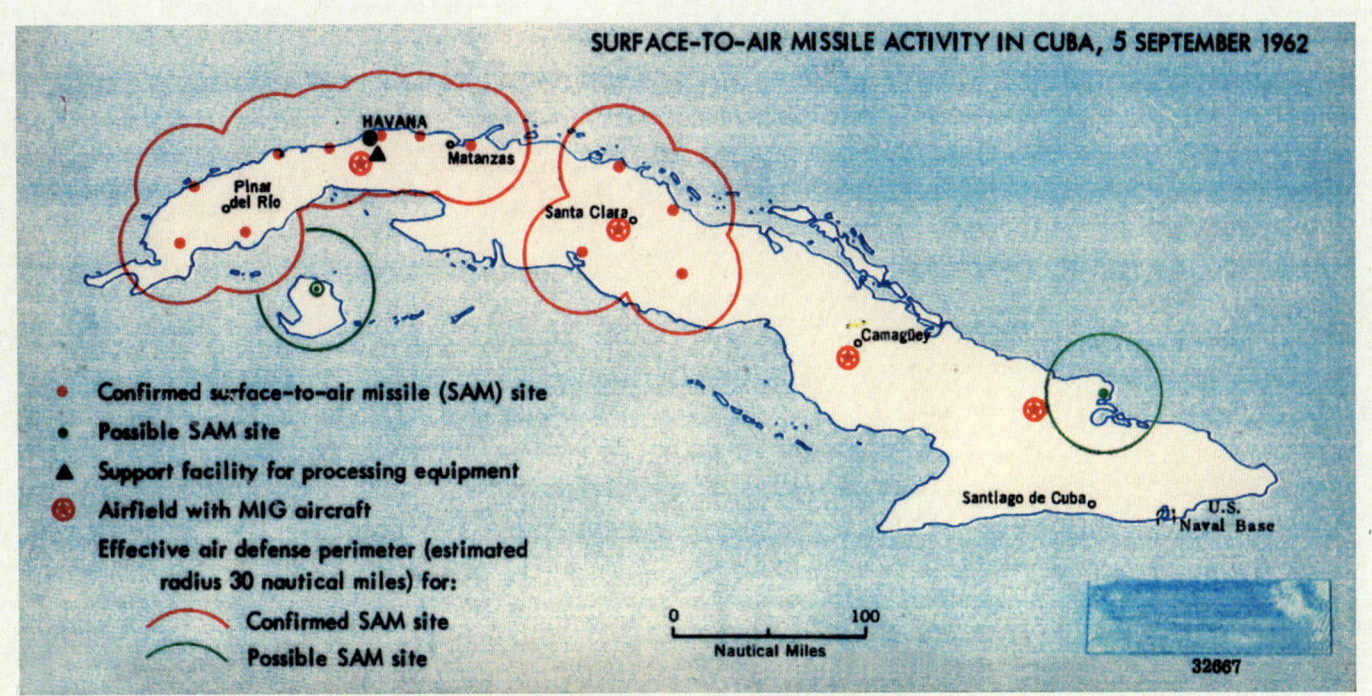

SURFACE-TO-AIR MISSILE ACTIVITY IN CUBA, 5 SEPTEMBER 1962

ABOVE: In September 1962, routine U-2 spy plane flights over the island of Cuba detected air defence (SAM) sites indicative of high-value targets, their locations are indicated on this map. (USAF)

Without credible value, the consequences of provocation were destabilising.

In its summary of a conference on June 16, 1959, a report noted that "The President said one thing…bothering him a great deal (which was) the plan to put IRBMs (in Europe). If…Cuba had been penetrated by the Communists, and then began getting arms and missiles from them, we would… look on such developments with the gravest concern and…it would be imperative for us to take positive action, even offensive military action…He wondered if we were not simply being provocative."

During Khrushchev's visit to the US three months later the Soviet Premier tossed a side comment to US labour union leader Victor Reuther, asking: "How would you feel if there were Soviet military bases in Mexico and Canada?" To which Reuther replied: "Who is keeping you from having them? Set them up!"

By the time Bolshakov was opening the clandestine link with Khrushchev, in September 1961 the Soviet Premier was planning to address the Party Congress and had already calmed hawks in the Praesidium over highly secret plans to put IRBMs in Cuba. After the Bay of Pigs fiasco five months previously, Moscow planned to deploy their SS-4 and SS-5 missiles to the Caribbean island where they would pose a similar threat to the United States as Jupiter and Thor missiles did to Russia. Khrushchev had managed to get that deferred but had lost ground to hard-liners in the process.

Meanwhile, the Berlin stand-off rumbled on and despite Kennedy's outward optimism for public consumption there was increasing belligerence in the open statements from Khrushchev, eager to please his detractors. Asked to craft a plan for attacking the Soviet Union should the need arise General Maxwell Taylor reviewed a policy proposal titled *Strategic Air Planning and Berlin*. Put together by Bundy's protégé Carl Kaysen, it offered an alternative to the SIOP-62 plan, described in chapter six.

Under SIOP-62 a massive nuclear strike would kill 54% of the Soviet population and Kennedy had already made it clear that he was reluctant to authorise such a plan over anything short of an all-out pre-emptive attack from Russia. If triggered by the Berlin crisis, Kaysen offered a scaled attack in which no more than a million civilians would perish. Marcus Raskin, a co-associate of Kaysen was deeply troubled, saying: "How does this make us any better than those who measured the gas ovens or the engineers who built the tracks for the death trains in Nazi Germany?"

Despite this being a modest proposal when compared to a lot of war scenarios evaluated in the Pentagon, to many civilians in the White House even that was inconceivable. Sorensen was thrown into a furious repost: "You're crazy," he said. "We shouldn't let guys like you around here!" Kennedy differed in his response and was interested in Kaysen's report, indicating that this was just the kind of option he sought and on September 19 convened with top military brass including the head of Strategic Air Command, General Thomas S Power.

Kennedy wanted to know what civilian targets could be removed from the list, whether it could exclude attacks on China and whether sites in Warsaw Pact countries had to be included. The original SIOP-62 attack plan had always included China since it considered that a response to an attack by Russia would be against all communist states. As a reciprocal, it was enshrined within NATO that an attack by Russia on any member state would be considered as an attack on them all.

In the event that tensions increased, Kennedy also wanted to know whether a first strike against the Soviet Union could take out Russia's long-range firepower before it could respond. And what sort of damage that would cause in Western Europe. Kennedy wanted definitive answers, declaring: "I am concerned over my ability to control our military effort once a war begins. I assume I can stop the strategic attack at any time, should I receive word that the enemy has capitulated. Is that correct?"

Decisions balanced between military advice, civilian caution and political

ABOVE: Fidel Castro had led a revolution to overthrow the Batista regime and sought interest in Russian offers for aid, including military support after the failed Bay of Pigs invasion by the CIA and Cuban exiles in April 1961. (CIA)

CHAPTER EIGHT

ABOVE: Moscow fostered close links with Castro, sending its first spaceman Yuri Gagarin to the country to further cooperation and links between the two countries. (Novosti)

expediency were hard to make and Kennedy was aware of the hawkish mentality in the Pentagon. Gen Power had served as deputy chief of operations during the firebombing of Japanese cities and the dropping of the two atomic bombs, urging a strong line and uncompromising in advising the President: "The time of our greatest danger of a Soviet surprise attack is now and during the coming year. If a general atomic war is inevitable, the US should strike first."

Power had been the stimulant to General LeMay's hard line approach to the use of strategic air power and nuclear weapons and he turned persuasively to achieve the same result with the President. Recalling Kennedy's election campaign call for a massive increase in US missiles, Power reminded the President that absence of evidence is not evidence of absence. The Soviets may have many more missiles than we can see, he said. Satellite photographs could not show concealed rockets, he believed.

This did not convince Kennedy, perhaps because he knew all along that the missile-gap theory was a myth and had already sought to roll back on initial plans very early in the year to support Pentagon demands for excessive deployment of US missiles. Nitze advised caution over the use of nuclear weapons, believing that their use would likely precipitate a full response from the Soviet Union. But he was not averse to a first strike to achieve strategic gain.

Rusk brought it all into perspective when he remarked that "The first side to use nuclear weapons will carry a very grave responsibility and endure heavy consequences before the rest of the world." As if to drive home the grim reality, on October 30 Russia tested the largest nuclear bomb ever detonated. With a yield of 50MT it was more than twice as powerful as the largest nuclear bomb deployed operationally by the United States. Scaled back from a theoretical yield of 100MT, it was a test never repeated and the Russian weapon was never deployed.

CHECKPOINT CHARLIE

With an uptick in armed forces deployed by the United States and all the military contingencies announced during his TV broadcast of July 25 now taking hold, Kennedy braced the administration for a furious response from Moscow. He now had the recommendations covering a suitable response to a series of possible steps the Russians might take over Berlin, how to react and with what level of force.

Known as National Security Action Memorandum No 109, it was agreed by the President and senior officials on October 20. Should the Russians interfere with traffic on the autobahn, platoons of soldiers would provide escort and allied fighters would take to the skies. If the Russians blocked access and persisted, general mobilisation would begin with economic embargoes imposed on land and at sea.

A third level would see armoured divisions sent to West Berlin with air strikes on Warsaw Pact airfields to suppress supporting actions from Soviet allies. Finally, enhanced diplomatic pressure would bring the use of conventional weapons in to play before the use of tactical nuclear weapons preceding general all-out war. These four stages would define how the West would respond. The memorandum was circulated to NATO members.

To concerns among US military commanders in Europe, Kennedy responded that "our nuclear deterrent will not be credible to the Soviets unless they are convinced of NATO's readiness to become engaged on a lesser level of violence and are thereby made to realise the great risks of escalation to nuclear war."

What Kennedy now decided to do was breath-taking in its implication and brilliant in its political value. He would upstage the Soviet Premier by publicly declaring the full potential of US military power, conventional and nuclear. By openly showing how strong the US arsenal had become it would counter Soviet claims of superior force and rebalance the agenda by challenging the Russians to deny that its ideological opponent now had the upper hand on policy options.

It was put together by Pentagon analyst Daniel Ellsberg. Unaware of the back-door channels with Bolshakov and others, Ellsberg asked Kaysen whether it would be preferable to have that sent to Khrushchev by intermediaries. That was not the point, Kennedy wanted to have the message sent not only in plain speech to an audience at home but to critics abroad and to all the Warsaw Pact countries.

To reduce its gravitas and to avoid interpretation that this was a belligerent challenge to Moscow direct from the White House, Kennedy had the Deputy Secretary of Defense, Roswell Gilpatric make that announcement the following day. After declaring that "this nation has a nuclear retaliatory force of such lethal power that any enemy move which brought it into play would be an act of self-destruction on his part," Gilpatric went through just how potent that force was, establishing that "a sneak attack could not effectively disarm us."

What happened on the following day brought the two superpowers close to the brink of war. Fuming at Khrushchev's statement that there was now no need to impose an end-of-year deadline for a separate East German peace treaty,

ABOVE: On several occasions, the Cuban revolutionaries attempted to plead their cause and establish stronger relations with the United States. Here Castro is making a speech at the United Nations Assembly in New York in 1960. (UN)

74 JFK – A LIFE REMEMBERED

CUBA

> "The Soviet Premier was playing a very dangerous game, appearing as two different people to separate audiences."

ABOVE: The United States had deployed Jupiter missiles to within striking distance of targets in Russia, the Kremlin asserting the right to do the same to North America by basing a similar capability in Cuba. (US Army)

Ulbricht's police began spot-checking civilians in violation of the four-power agreement for access across the sectors. He then decided to stiffen checkpoint crossings and to harass US officials by delaying them. A strong reaction to that had been encouraged by Lucius Clay.

During the evening of October 22 and with encouragement from Clay, senior US Embassy staffer E Allan Lightner Jr and his wife Dorothy were stopped at Checkpoint Charlie on their way to the theatre in East Berlin and denied rightful passage. Along with General Watson, Clay set up headquarters at the US consulate on the Clayallee, a former Luftwaffe building from where he would conduct operations.

When the tension began to rise, Clay ordered four M48 tanks up from McNair Barracks about 16km (10 miles) from Checkpoint Charlie. Unsheathing the bayonets on their rifles, the US platoon marched inexorably across the barrier, around the obstacles and entered Soviet territory, the East German guards slowly retreating backwards.

As the four tanks arrived, Dorothy Lightner was asked to get out the car and withdraw as two infantry squads set up station on the Friedrichstrasse. To emphasise a point, escorted by armed troops Lightner drove forward two blocks, turned around and slowly returned back to the US side of the crossing.

Wanting to emphasise the point, Lightner again drove forward. This time East German guards blocked his way until the US platoon accompanied him and the guards stood aside, uncertain about what to do and reluctant to start World War Three. His return back across coincided with the arrival of a Soviet official apologising profusely for the mistake.

Thus empowered, Lightner was joined by a second car, the two driving right up the Friedrichstrasse to the Unter den Linden as far as the Brandenburg Gate, turning left and back through Checkpoint Charlie. The situation was quickly brought to Kennedy, annoyed that this avoidable excursion into East Berlin and the strident reaction of Lucius Clay could undo his attempt to secure a covert information line with Khrushchev.

Over the next several days various excursions to the checkpoint were made and passage allowed under the terms of the agreement, but the standoff had brought both sides close to a firefight with more US tanks moving up to face down Russian armour brought in from the surrounding area. By the end of October, the situation had calmed and with backdoor communications providing secure means of an exchange, both Kennedy and Khrushchev agreed to withdraw their respective forces.

In a conference held at Los Alamos Scientific Laboratory September 3-5, 1989 it was revealed that the Davy Crockett tactical nuclear weapon had been deployed to West Germany. With a range of up to 4km (2.5 miles) it had a yield of 20 tonnes of TNT and could be fired from a recoilless rifle, an elongated tube mounted on a tripod. Both sides were poised for an exchange with tanks and armoured vehicles which, if begun could have rapidly escalated into a battle at Checkpoint Charlie.

MISSILES ON CUBA

Isolated as separate incidents in time, the Berlin crisis melded seamlessly into what history would record as the Cuban Missile Crisis. Alarmed at how rapidly the Berlin crisis had escalated, Khrushchev sought to

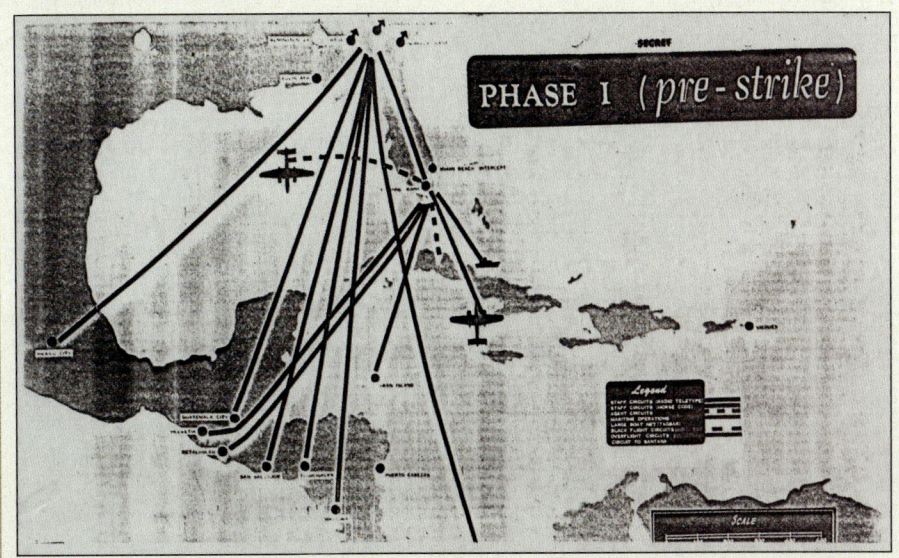

ABOVE: Fearful of a surge in the overthrow of Latin American countries by revolutionary communists, the US Department of Defense planned a series of attacks as a precursor to invasion, should that be decided, as displayed on this declassified map of an air assault. (CIA)

CHAPTER EIGHT

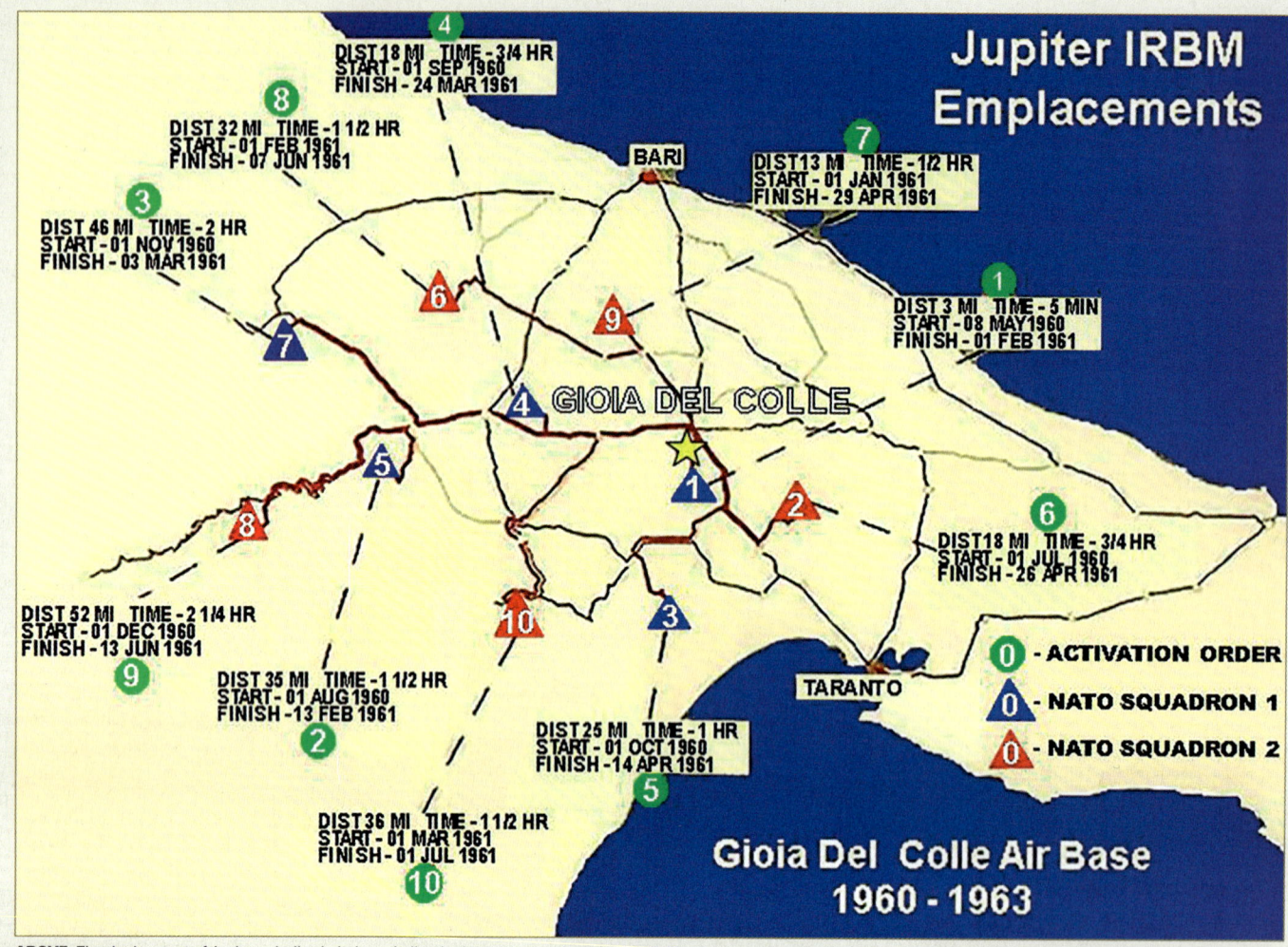

ABOVE: The deployment of Jupiter missiles in Italy, a similar deployment was also set up in Turkey, both countries being strong members of NATO. (Author's archive)

prepare Soviet forces for a potential war with the United States. To prepare for an attack into West Germany, the Russians laid an oil pipeline up to the border for refuelling Soviet armour should it conduct a panzer strike into Western Europe. Tactical nuclear weapons were redeployed, and several improvements were made to airfields, all of which was reported back to Kennedy.

Throughout, Khrushchev used the backdoor channels to maintain a level of conciliation with the White House, choosing to smooth differences quietly while openly throwing a loud and rambunctious tirade of abuse at the West. Before Christmas 1961 and less than two months after the standoff at Checkpoint Charlie, quietly and completely unknown to the Americans at the time, Khrushchev was putting final touches to his plan to deploy nuclear weapons, medium-range bombers, and ballistic missiles in Cuba.

Challenged at home by aggressive elements in the Kremlin, the Soviet Premier chafed at the way he had been pressured by Ulbricht over a peace treaty for East Germany, which appeared to him to be receding beyond the political horizon, and the embarrassment of having been faced down by Kennedy over Berlin. Needing to show strength and purpose, the delayed plan for missiles to Cuba could wait no longer.

BELOW: US Defense Secretary McElroy inspecting the Jupiter production line. Taking several hours to prepare for launch, Jupiter missiles were not a first-strike weapon, their preparation for flight being readily visible, but they provided an added threat to Moscow. (ABMA)

Quietly, Khrushchev sought to reassure his critics and shared with officials a belief that the United States would never resort to nuclear war, claiming: "I know for certain that Kennedy doesn't have a strong background, nor, generally speaking, does he have the courage to stand up to a serious challenge." As his son would later recall, Khrushchev believed that Kennedy would "make a fuss, make more of a fuss, and then agree" over missiles on Cuba.

> "Khrushchev was under fire from hard-line Kremlin types blaming him for being too soft on the Americans, for not demanding stiffer conditions over Berlin and for stalling stronger moves to challenge the US over its expanding strategic nuclear capabilities."

To some extent there was truth in that. Kennedy accepted that the Soviet Union would press for the withdrawal of non-Russian troops from Berlin. Khrushchev proposed a United Nations force of blue-helmet troops to replace British, French, and American forces but that was rebuffed by the White House. Referring back to the speech of July 25, 1961 where Kennedy had referred to West Berlin and not the city as a whole, Khrushchev and Ulbricht saw that as tacit recognition that eventually Berlin would be united.

At home too, Kennedy faced dissent over the division of Berlin, this symbolic edifice to German hegemony in two world wars where a bizarre treaty signed in 1945 had divided up this one place in all East Germany, so far from the border with West Germany. Chairman of the Senate Foreign Relations Committee William Fulbright expressed the views of many when he claimed that, in his view "the Russians have the power to close it in any case…Next week if they chose to…without violating any treaty," adding that "I don't understand why the East Germans don't close their border, because I think they have a right to close it."

As political in-fighting rumbled on, the demands from Moscow began to increase, fuelled in part by Khrushchev's new-found assertiveness that he was about to challenge Kennedy in the most direct way possible. The Cuba missiles plan was growing in size and complexity, all tightly controlled with high levels of secrecy surrounding a major operation involving ships to carry the vast array of equipment all the way to the Caribbean island.

The US had a programme of surveillance over Cuba and from early 1962 had noted an increase in Soviet ships delivering supplies to the island. What Kennedy did not know was that in late 1961 Khrushchev had agreed to supply Castro with more surface-to-air missile (SAM) batteries for defence against air attack from the United States. Air defence missiles had already been delivered to Cuba, but Castro wanted more and as part of his long-term plan to build up military forces on the island, the Russians concurred.

But Khrushchev had his problems when in March 1962 pro-Soviet members of Castro's inner council were ousted as the government moved closer to China, which was in its own ideological spat with Moscow. Realising the threat to pro-Soviet alignment, Khrushchev accelerated plans to give Castro what he asked for and that expanded plans for equipping Cuba with nuclear-tipped missiles. The missiles programme was now seen as a way of cementing relations with Moscow, something his detractors in the Kremlin had sought all along.

The scale of the munitions-supply route to Cuba became so great that US intelligence was now well aware that something big was going on, that deliveries were more than mere supplies and that the increase in construction equipment warranted further investigation. But these developments had a more strategic importance than the military threat to the United States implied by their deployment.

Khrushchev now believed that if such missiles were set up and announced to the West, he could trade their removal for the withdrawal of American, British, and French troops from West Berlin, absorbing those sectors into a unified city under East German rule, placating the troublesome Ulbricht. Khrushchev knew that Russia had few intercontinental missiles of its own capable of striking the US from Soviet territory and that the only threat to US cities would come from intermediate range types placed close to America.

After the stand-off over Checkpoint Charlie, it was the only strong card to play and a delegation from Moscow arrived in Cuba during late spring 1962 to plan sites, access roads, fuel storage facilities, and equipment dumps. Officially the plan was known as Operation Anadyr, after the river that flows into the Bering Sea, and it was officially signed off by Khrushchev on July 7 involving more than 40,000 troops from Russia and some from Warsaw Pact countries. The entire operation was conducted in secret, none of the personnel

BELOW: Thor missiles were deployed to the UK for a similar role to the Jupiter rockets, this US Air Force programme ensuring added back-up. (USAF)

CHAPTER EIGHT

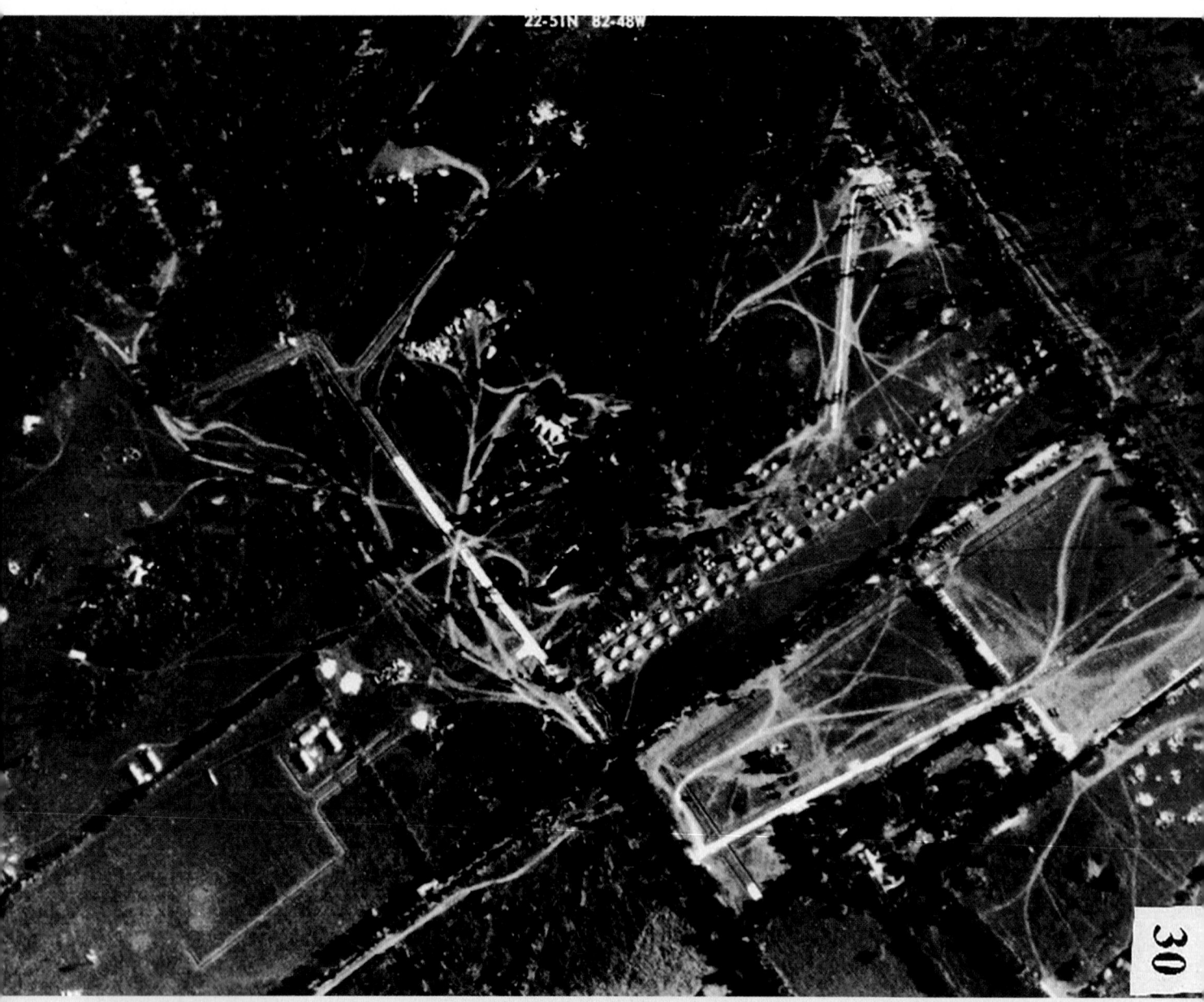

ABOVE: Reconnaissance photographs from U-2 spy plane flights over Cuba revealed increased military activity and troops bivouacked at locations adjacent to newly installed air defence systems, raising concerns about Russia's planned deployments. (CIA)

deployed knowing where they were going or why and they had been issued with cold-weather clothing and equipment to mask their real destination.

Khrushchev's plan involved 24 medium-range SS-4 rockets, 16 intermediate-range SS-5 missiles, 42 Il-28 bombers, a single fighter wing, two tank battalions and air-defence missiles at eight sites already agreed by Castro and all to be in place by the end of 1962. The bombers threatened all of Florida and the SS-4s could strike as far north as Boston and west to New Mexico but the SS-5s could hit almost all of the 48 contiguous states and all the US ICBM sites. What was perhaps most worrying was that these offensive weapons were only appropriate for a first strike since they would be exposed to attack on open and unprotected launch sites.

General intelligence about Soviet deployments in Cuba became common knowledge at the CIA and this was brought to Kennedy on August 10 by CIA chief John A McCone when he warned that it appeared that ballistic missiles were to be set up on the island. The Soviets denied that and in a personal message to Kennedy insisted: "We have no bases in Cuba, and we do not intend to establish any." The message was repeated to Robert Kennedy.

Other issues concerned Kennedy. With conflicting verdicts on his political performance over Berlin and an upcoming Congressional election for 39 of the 100 Senate seats and all of the House votes up for grabs on November 6, it was no time to declare another emergency to challenge his authority or that of the Democrats. But events would rapidly overtake the campaign. It was, nevertheless, one reason why Kennedy wanted to keep a lid on what had all the makings of another international crisis.

On the domestic front, no real progress had been made over his New Frontier programmes, a cornerstone of his election speech and Kennedy was worried over his administration's mid-term report card about to be marked at the ballot box. Nevertheless, further intelligence information produced the need for a secondary plan and Kennedy sought a wider set of options over Cuba other than an escalation to war.

Accepting Kennedy's reluctance to engage with Moscow on a nuclear exchange, some national security advisers had a further step. Suppose, they said, Khrushchev refuses to back down and takes West Berlin by military force. Instead of escalating to a confrontation first by conventional means and then by a nuclear exchange, the President could respond by taking Cuba. For which of course there would need to be a fully developed plan for an invasion.

This had particular attraction for Kennedy. With many US intelligence assets watching Che Guevara, the Argentinian Marxist revolutionary in Guatemala and strong supporter of Castro, US agents tracked his visit to Moscow on August 30. Fearing that this was part of an escalating move by Khrushchev to recruit client states in the Caribbean and South America, Kennedy was

CUBA

briefed on what appeared to be a complex web of interconnected moves all linked back to the Berlin crisis.

EXCOMM

Concern over Cuba sponsored several plans produced at the Pentagon where Curtis LeMay laid out options for a bombing campaign prior to an invasion. Far removed from the half-hearted attempt at the Bay of Pigs 16 months earlier, this was to be a fully supported assault following an intensive bombing campaign to destroy military installations. It became clear that the Kennedy administration had to act when on August 31 Republican Senator Kenneth Keating, with an eye on the upcoming election, publicly declared that he believed the Russians would be putting missiles into Cuba.

Keating was correct. Two days earlier a U-2 spy flight over Cuba, one of many conducted since the Bay of Pigs, brought photographic evidence of eight SAM sites on Cuba of the type designed to take down high-flying aircraft. On receiving this information, Kennedy told the CIA to "put it in the box and nail it shut." But the genie was already out. Media reports began to circulate, and comment was sought but ignored by officials. There was no time to wait and be dragged, tail-first into obfuscation. Additional analysis showed that Russian fighter aircraft were already on the island.

Seeking to construct a public statement to allay fears and ward off accusations of inaction from the Republicans, particularly those standing for re-election, Kennedy convened a meeting of top advisers in the Cabinet Room at the White House on Tuesday, September 4, 1962. In the conversation that ensued, Robert Kennedy mentioned the issue of the Monroe Doctrine which would, he implied, resonate with the American public and gain their support for ousting any Soviet presence in Cuba.

The Monroe Doctrine had been set as a pillar of US foreign policy since introduced by President James Monroe on December 2, 1823. It decreed that no European colonisation was to be allowed in the Western Hemisphere and that the United States was policeman to that edict, a cardinal point taught in every American school. Robert Kennedy believed that the outrage at Soviet 'colonisation' of Cuba would resonate with the US voter, but it was disregarded as being irrelevant at the meeting on September 4.

Determined to prepare a press statement on the rumours, the meeting adjourned for Robert to prepare a draft before re-convening later that day where the discussion focused on the amount of intelligence to be revealed publicly. JFK was particularly interested to know from LeMay how easy it would be to destroy the SAM sites and the missiles, the reassuring answer implying a low-level attack below radar coverage.

The meeting broke for a briefing to Congressional leaders who learned that as of this date, in addition to the eight SAM sites the Russians had 60 fighter aircraft on Cuba, none of which were the more challenging MiG-21s. Kennedy emphasised that no

BELOW: Russia planned to place SS-4 rockets in partially concealed locations on Cuba to threaten most of Florida and the southern states, this example preserved in a Russian museum. (Leonidi/wikkicommons)

> "The entrenched positions of the two leaders over Berlin appeared to have calmed the 'hawks' and satisfied the 'doves', those who sought conciliation and co-existence."

www.keymilitary.com

CHAPTER EIGHT

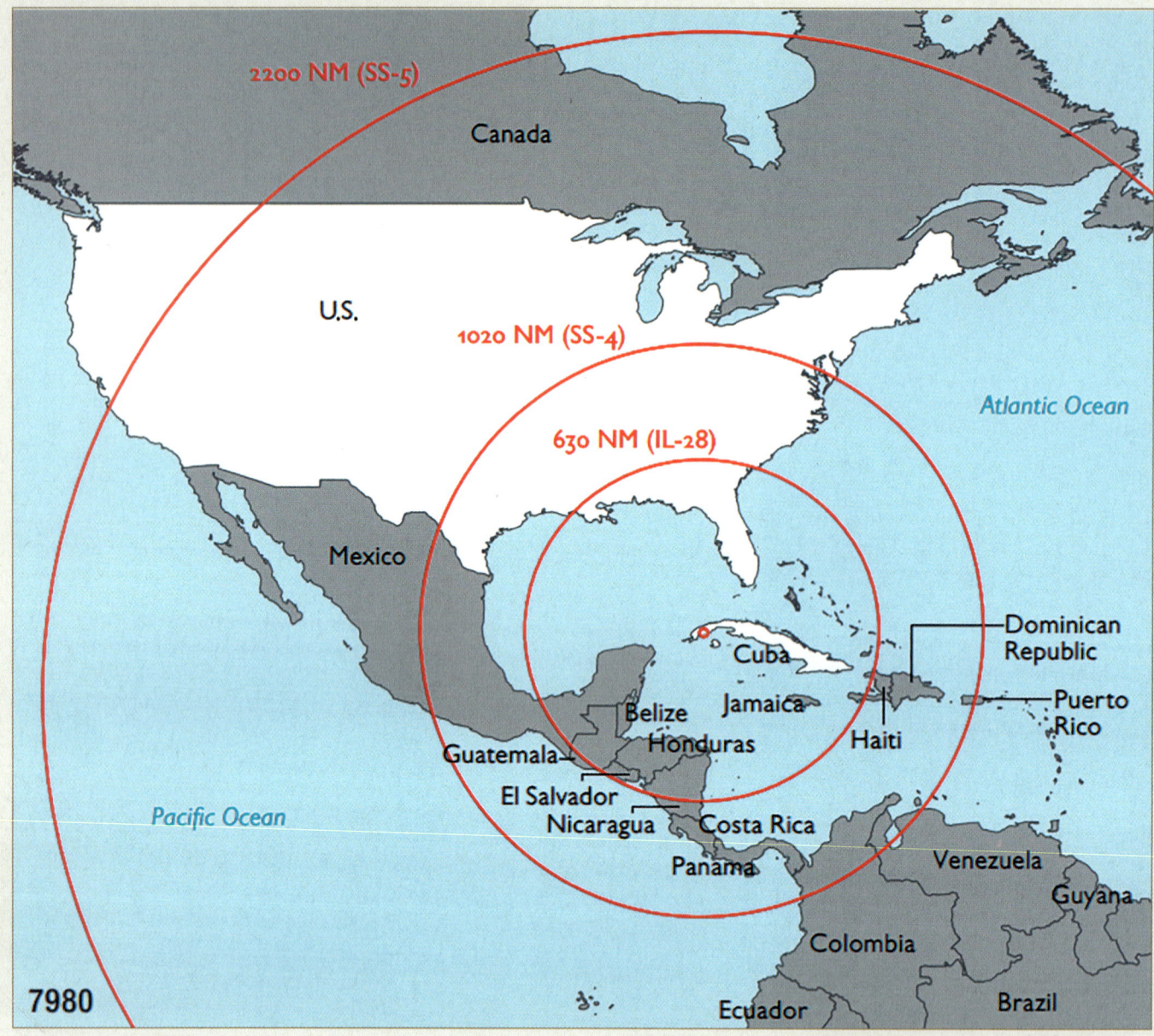

ABOVE: Along with the SS-4 and the SS-5, the Russians also planned to deliver a force of medium-range Il-28 bombers to Cuba, the effective radius of each delivery system shown here. (DIA)

'offensive' weapons had yet been seen in U-2 photos, only 'defensive' weaponry. But the possibility of a spy plane being shot down was real, the Russian SAMs being capable of hitting any aircraft up to 48km (30 miles) away or to 30,480m (100,000ft) in altitude.

Concerned as to whether he intended to intervene at this juncture, Kennedy reassured the group that in what he knew to have been installed "We are not talking about nuclear warheads…I could not see, under present conditions, the United States intervening. It would be a major military operation." And when comparing it to other stress point around the globe, he cautioned that "we just have to try to keep all of that in perspective."

When asked about the possibility of a blockade, Kennedy believed that would be ineffective. On which point, he was well aware that the use of the word 'blockade' implied a declaration of war, whereas 'quarantine' was an acceptable use of diplomatic language to assert a denial of access without implying a hostile act on another country. Semantics to the uninitiated but the hinge-line for conflict in the nuanced world of international power politics. But the real world kicked back in when JFK and his brother briefed a smaller group on the need for supplemental funds to call up a further 150,000 reservists.

Later, Robert Kennedy met with Soviet Ambassador Anatoly Dobrynin who relayed a message from Khrushchev to reassure the Americans that there were no missiles or any other form of offensive weapon on Cuba. Dobrynin would also make this claim to the US Ambassador to the UN, Adlai Stevenson that "only defensive weapons are being supplied" to Cuba.

The day ended when Salinger read the statement to invited reporters, at pains to

ABOVE: Designated SS-4 *Sandalwood* by NATO, this medium-range rocket has been set on display in Cuba as a reminder of events in October 1962. (Suvoro/wikicommons)

point out that there was "no evidence of any organised combat force in Cuba from any Soviet bloc country." In addition, it noted that "the Castro regime will not be allowed to export its aggressive purposes by use of force or by the threat of force." At 7:35pm, the President went for a swim in the indoor pool surrounded by a mural of the US Virgin Islands and recently completed by Bernard Lamotte.

Seeking to remove fears of an imminent invasion of Cuba in rumours put about by Castro, on September 12 Kennedy had charged him of "a frantic effort to bolster his regime," claiming that "unilateral military intervention on the part of the United States cannot be…justified." Which was true of the situation as it existed on that day, but the Russian cargo ship *Poltava* was closing fast on the island.

Just three days later, on September 15 *Poltava* docked at the Cuban port of Mariel with the first SS-4 missiles on board but there was little air intelligence to know that at this date. Within two days the missiles had been unloaded and eight delivered to San Cristóbal where they would be based.

ABOVE: Larger than the SS-4, from bases in Cuba the SS-5 *Skean* posed a threat to almost all the continental United States. Both missiles took time to prepare for launch and could have led to a misinterpretation of activity leading to a first-strike by the US. (Novosti)

By this time US Tactical Air Command had drawn up plans for a coordinated air attack on Cuba and the initial steps had been taken to provide logistical support and prepare for a strike.

On September 19, Kennedy was briefed by the intelligence community with news that another ship, the *Omsk* had arrived and that after offloading the vessel was riding high in the water, allowing analysts to

ABOVE: Spy plane images of the San Cristobal site where launchers and missile trailers could be seen, the radius of curvature on access roads indicating the size of missiles planned for deployment. (DIA)

CHAPTER EIGHT

ABOVE: With his back to the camera Jack Kennedy talks to his brother Bobby about the unfolding crisis as uncertainty pervades the decision process. (NARA)

determine the weight of offloaded materiel. The next day the Senate approved the use of military force to curb Cuban aggression by 86:1 and the House of Representatives passed a bill to cut off aid to any country transporting goods of any kind to Cuba.

The military plan was presented to LeMay on September 27 when he was briefed on all the separate strands of an attack, preparations which would be ready by October 20 should they be required. Such a response appeared more likely on September 28 when US Navy reconnaissance aircraft secured photographs of 10 large crates on the Russian ship *Kaisermov*. These contained Il-28 bombers, first generation jets which by this date had been completely removed from the Soviet Air Force. But they were not capable of carrying nuclear bombs.

After receiving a set of trigger-points for military action, Robert Kennedy conveyed

ABOVE: ExComm meetings provided focused and channelled discussion over options about the gathering war clouds as (left to right), Jack Kennedy, Dean Rusk, and Robert McNamara mull options. (NARA)

ABOVE: Relations with the Russian Ambassador Andrei Gromyko (facing camera) were more cordial than those between the White House and the Kremlin, the Soviet representative having been uninformed about the missile deployments until told by the Americans. (NARA)

concerns of the President regarding Operation Mongoose, a highly classified, covert CIA operation to overthrow the Castro regime which had been sanctioned by Kennedy on November 30, 1961. Set in place after a meeting with Robert Kennedy three weeks earlier, JFK wanted a permanent rolling programme to wear down the Castro regime, depose Cuba's dictator and return the island to US control by an approved successor. It was run out of a top secret location near Miami, Florida.

As Russian technicians worked with Cuban labourers to set up the installations from Russia, on October 14 a U-2 piloted by Richard Heyser, which had been grounded due to poor weather, brought back the first hard evidence. They showed all but one of the remaining 24 missile sites across Cuba. Late on the evening of the following day the details had been verified but the President was not informed by Bundy until 8:45am the following morning.

Acting quickly, Kennedy called a meeting of about 14 key specialists and advisers, that meeting getting under way by 11:45am.

This meeting became the first of what would henceforth be known as ExComm – the Executive Committee which would form whenever events dictated a decisive decision. During the session Robert Kennedy expressed surprise at the news and John McCloy, a lawyer in JFK's confidence suggested the use of force to take out the missiles. Briefers testified that they did not believe any of the weapons had been armed but more information was urgently required. An additional six U-2 flights were conducted this day.

RISING TENSION

JFK was concerned about progress with Mongoose, and this was conveyed to senior military officers the following day, Robert Kennedy conveying a general desire to roll together the response to the Soviet missiles and the regime change in Cuba. On October 16 the second ExComm meeting convened at

ABOVE: The strategic capacity of the United States to strike the Soviet Union was overwhelming, the most survivable element of the nuclear triad being the Polaris missile deployed at sea. (USN)

under similar circumstances! At this, JFK recoiled, reminding the group that such an action would not be compatible with "American principles" and directed that all attention should go to the quarantine plan.

When ExComm adjourned at 5:10pm, JFK told Sorensen that he was cancelling all appointments in support of the Congressional mid-term elections. Earlier in the day the ExComm minutes show that Kennedy had agreed that "at an appropriate time we would have to acknowledge that we were willing to take strategic missiles out of Turkey and Italy if this issue was raised by the Russians…but he was firm in saying we should only make such a proposal in the future." Kennedy also told Sorensen that he would not make a final decision over airstrike or quarantine in the speech he was preparing for two days hence until one final deliberation through ExComm.

Kennedy was still deeply concerned at the military threat to the United States. The National Intelligence Estimate for October 20 showed 16 SS-4 launchers were operational with a capability to launch at eight hours' notice, that there were 22 Il-28 bombers, 39 MiG-21s and 62 fighters with lesser capability, 24 air-defence SAM sites and three cruise missile sites for coastal defence, with 12 Komar-class cruise-missile equipped patrol boats. Alarmingly, a nuclear warhead storage bunker had been identified at a missile site with no indication that a weapon was there.

At 10am on October 21, Rusk and McNamara met with JFK who gave final approval for the quarantine plan over an airstrike. The air attack concept was discussed by Kennedy in the Oval Office

6:30pm to hear that the latest analysis would have the missiles armed "within two weeks." Both Kennedys defined a three-prong solution involving initial contact with Castro failing, after which there would be a blockade of weapons followed by a direct attack on Cuba.

October 17 brought worse news. The first site for the longer-range SS-5 missiles had been detected and two more would soon be noted but no missiles of this type would ever arrive on the island, although that was not known at the time. Moreover, Bolshakov conveyed a message to Robert Kennedy that Khrushchev again wanted him to know that no offensive missiles would be sent to Cuba. By the time it reached JFK he had already been briefed on the day's news.

The following day's ExComm meeting heard a recommendation from the Joint Chiefs of Staff to begin air strikes, but Robert Kennedy raised the moral issue, noting later in his diary of events that "more time was spent on this moral question during the first five days than on any other single matter." For JFK, it was the question of a "Pearl Harbor in reverse" but Acheson told the President that he was "being silly" and that it was "unworthy of him to talk that way."

On this day, much discussion surrounded the possibility of a quarantine of Cuba and most members of ExComm appeared to support the idea but during the sessions opinion began to harden against that. Robert Kennedy was concerned about the legalities and contacted his deputy, Nicholas deB Katzenbach to get advice, those matters also being checked by Leonard C Meeker from the State Department. Legal opinion was varied, and nobody appeared able to provide a definitive answer.

On October 19, the differences became quite stark, and Kennedy wanted clear options that were not forthcoming so ExComm decided to set up separate working groups which would provide better focus on specific aspects. Over the day opinion that previously favoured air strikes began to migrate across to the quarantine camp and on through that night Sorensen worked on a speech which would be given by JFK announcing that course of action.

However, the hawks were not done and during the meeting on October 20 JFK learned that the airstrike option was not a surgical attack on targeted sites but a major, all-out attack on Cuba. One member of the Joint Chiefs advocating the use of nuclear weapons in such a raid defended that by claiming the Russians would do the same

ABOVE: On October 23, 1962 President Kennedy signed the quarantine order aimed at preventing Russian ships from reaching the island. (NARA)

CHAPTER EIGHT

ABOVE: Each Washington-class nuclear-powered submarine carried 16 Polaris missiles which, with an intermediate range required the submarine to be close to Russia for a strike on planned targets. (USN)

with General Walter C Sweeney, head of Tactical Air Command who informed the President that no more than 90% of the missile sites could be destroyed. There was risk. Although placing the airstrike plan second to a quarantine, JFK instructed Sweeney to have his force ready for operations from the following morning.

Concerned about having the right people in place to convey the appropriate messages, halfway through the ExComm meeting that began at 2:30pm, Kennedy broke away to converse with Robert Lovett, a trusted confidante, seeking opinion as to who should handle negotiations over the crisis at the United Nations. Lovett suggested John McCloy, JFK agreed and had him immediately flown back from Germany to act as assistant to Adlair Stevenson.

During the meeting, Admiral George Andersen briefed ExComm on procedures for handling the quarantine, explaining that each ship approaching the line of demarcation would have to stop for boarding and inspection. If it did not a shot would be fired across its bow and if there was still no response, a shot would disable the ship's rudder. Kennedy was concerned that this might unintentionally destroy the boat but at the end of the meeting he was resigned to the reality that "the biggest danger lay in taking no action."

At the end of the day reports were circulated to Kennedy that three newspapers had the story and would publish on the following day. Kennedy himself called Max Frankel at the *New York Times* and Philip Graham at the *Washington Post* while McNamara called John Hay Whitney at the *New York Herald Tribune*. All three agreed to hold the story in the national interest and to prevent inadvertent escalation.

EYEBALL TO EYEBALL

At 10:55am on October 22 the State Department authorised diplomatic posts around the world to brief foreign heads of government over the quarantine decision. Five minutes later Dean Acheson called De Gaulle who responded: "it is exactly what I would have done…You may tell your President that France will support him."

By noon day a massive alert of US SAC bombers began with all forces equipped with live nuclear weapons. About 13% of the strategic B-52 force was constantly airborne and 183 medium-range B-47 bombers were dispersed to 33 civilian and military airfields. US air defence units dispersed 161 combat aircraft to 16 bases in nine hours. ICBM forces went on alert and Polaris submarines departed for preassigned locations from where they could launch their missiles.

At 2:14pm the Joint Chiefs notified all US military forces worldwide that readiness was increased to DEFCON 3 with the US Air Force on a 15-min warning to mobilisation, DEFCON 2 implying conflict could begin within six hours, DEFCON 1 that a nuclear attack was imminent or had begun.

Throughout the afternoon Kennedy worked to reassure allies and NATO countries that unity was essential but that he was prepared to go all the way. During the late afternoon Rusk handed Ambassador Dobrynin a copy of the message Kennedy was to deliver on national TV during that evening. It was the first Dobrynin had heard about missiles in Cuba and Rusk noted that: "he aged 10 years in front of my eyes."

Kennedy began his televised address at 7pm explaining "unmistakable evidence" of Russian missiles in Cuba, announcing a strict quarantine was being put in place. As he spoke,

ABOVE: Land-based Atlas missiles were not effective as quick reaction weapons despite their intercontinental range, this model here being one of the early A-series during test. (USAF)

22 air-defence fighters went airborne in case the Cubans reacted with sending bombers to the United States. Intelligence intercepted a communication from Khrushchev to Russian ships ordering them to ignore the quarantine. To Kennedy, Khrushchev hoped that "the United States government will display wisdom and renounce the actions pursued by you which may lead to catastrophic consequences for world peace."

October 23 saw a flurry of activity at the United Nations, accusations and recriminations flowing back and forth while Kennedy kept abreast of news that an enhanced flurry of coded messages had been sent to Russian ships heading for Cuba. Late in the day he received news that Soviet nuclear submarines were moving into the area. At 6:51pm Kennedy sent a reply to Khrushchev urging that he "show prudence and do nothing to allow events to make the situation more difficult."

Shortly after 7pm, Kennedy formally signed the quarantine order which was to begin at 10am the following day. Castro spoke to his people declaring that his country would never disarm, saying: "We still acquire the arms we feel like acquiring and we don't have to give an account to the imperialists" and that any potential inspectors must come "in battle array."

Throughout these episodes, Robert Kennedy played a significant role in connecting with his own group of contacts and informants and in providing alternative opinions to JFK who was beginning to show signs of fatigue and exasperation at the flow of events. After having had talks with Dobrynin, at 10:15am on October 24 he briefed JFK on those discussions and debated the President's idea of an immediate summit with Khrushchev, dismissing that as useless until the Soviet leader "first accepted US…determination in this matter."

As to the quarantine limit, after discussions with navy chiefs, Kennedy agreed to shorten the line to 804km (500 miles) rather than the original 1,290km (800 miles) after believing that even that reduced distance was "excessive." McNamara also briefed Kennedy on the start to navy reconnaissance flights over the island to keep a closer watch on ground activity, the first of 158 low-level missions flown by November 15. In response to US actions, Moscow placed Warsaw Pact forces on alert. In a poll on that October day, 84% of Americans favoured the quarantine but 20% believed it would lead to World War Three.

At 6am, October 24, intelligence landed on the President's desk that communist reaction to the quarantine order had openly resulted in a 'noncommittal statement' from Moscow and reports arrived with Kennedy that the Russian ships appeared to have slowed down, 16 of the 19 ships having reversed their course with only the tanker *Bucharest* appearing to sail on. But the President still had concerns, while Khrushchev met with US businessman William Knox for more than three hours and claimed that he would give orders to sink US warships if they enforced the quarantine.

At 9:35am, Robert spoke briefly with JFK and in reply to JFK's continuing concerns, noted that: "I just don't think there was any choice…if you hadn't acted you would have been impeached." Pausing reflectively for a moment, Kennedy replied "That's what

ABOVE: More effective than the Atlas missile was the massive Titan II with storable propellants, protected in underground silos and capable of delivering a devastating blow on targets in Russia with multi-megaton yield warheads. (USAF)

BELOW: Watched over by a US Navy HSS-1 Seabat helicopter, the Soviet submarine B-59 came close to starting World War Three when it almost fired a torpedo at the US aircraft carrier *Essex* before it was brought to the surface by depth charges. (USN)

> "Under SIOP-62 a massive nuclear strike would kill 54% of the Soviet population and Kennedy had already made it clear that he was reluctant to authorise such a plan over anything short of an all-out pre-emptive attack from Russia."

CHAPTER EIGHT

I think – I would have been impeached," defining the situation now hovering on a knife-edge as the hour neared at which the quarantine would come into effect.

ExComm met at 10am that day which Robert characterised as "the most trying, the most difficult and the most filled with tension." It was the pivotal point of the whole crisis as news came that a Soviet submarine had positioned itself between two Russian ships and was threatening the US aircraft carrier *Essex*. Small practice depth charges were being used to force the submarine to the surface. Unknown at the time, the political commissar on board the Soviet submarine ordered the captain to fire torpedoes at the *Essex*. He refused and in so doing probably saved the world from war.

At 10:15am news arrived that some of the Russian ships had stopped 'dead in the water'. Dean Rusk leaned over to McGeorge Bundy and said: "We're eyeball to eyeball, and I think the other fellow just blinked." But it was not over, as Khrushchev, probably sensing a standoff increased his bluster and threatened escalation. To stiffen US resolve, Kennedy authorised armed forces to go to DEFCON 2.

The following day tensions ebbed and flowed and in a syndicated piece, influential columnist Walter Lippman 'suggested' a "fast moving" agreement for the US to remove Jupiter missiles from Italy and Turkey if the Russians abandoned their plan to put missiles in Cuba. It was a public airing of secret discussions that had already been taking place between intermediaries. October 25 proved a turning point, but the following day Kennedy believed that a quarantine alone would not stop the missiles.

At 1pm on October 26 KGB Washington chief Alexander Fomin had lunch with State Department correspondent for ABC News, John Scali to muse over a plan whereby the US would pledge never to invade Cuba in exchange for the missiles. A note from Khrushchev arrived at 6pm declaring that he would pledge that no ships bound for Cuba are carrying weapons if the US agreed not to invade the island, the letter being considered by ExComm at 10pm that evening.

On the same day, Robert Kennedy had another in a series of secret meetings with Dobrynin at the Soviet Embassy and formally offered to introduce the US missiles in Italy and Turkey into the discussion. A lengthy series of exchanges, diplomatic messages and covert conversations ensued. At 9am on October 28 an open message from Khrushchev was broadcast on Radio Moscow verifying that the Soviet government had ordered that "further work at the building sites for the weapons" was to be discontinued and that missiles "which you describe as 'offensive'…(will be returned) to the Soviet Union."

It took some time for tensions to abate, Castro complaining that he had been "put

ABOVE: A P-2H Neptune of the US Navy patrols the seas and watches over a Soviet ship with crated Il-28 bombers on its deck. (USN)

BELOW: The 'game-theory' progressive sequence of decisions underpinning the war plan in response to Soviet missile on Cuba. (John Yaeger)

Cuban Missile Crisis Game Tree
A: The United States (President Kennedy)
B: The Soviet Union (Premier Khrushchev)

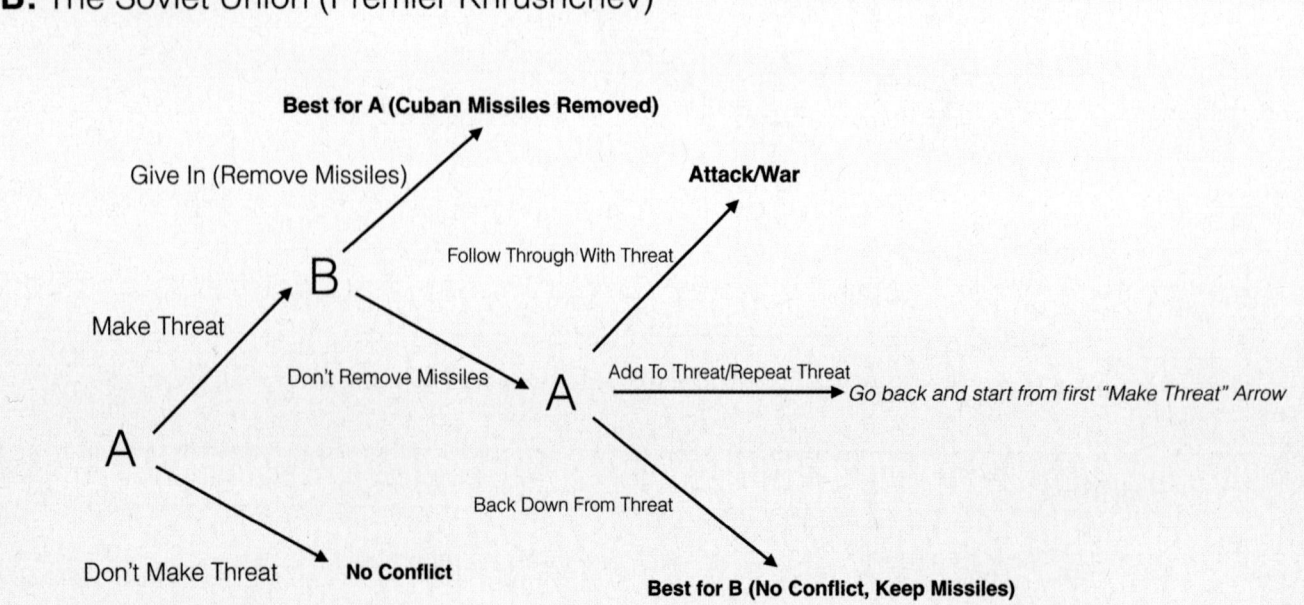

out to dry," Turkey chafing at losing a key asset with fellow NATO member Italy being circumspect about that. The US agreed not to invade Cuba and Khrushchev was one step closer to being ousted. Having seen to have failed in his adventures, within two years he was gone, by which time JFK had been assassinated.

That the world was saved an unimaginable and catastrophic nuclear war was largely due to Kennedy's determination to balance caution with firmness, to constrain a preference for overwhelming force in favour of discussion and negotiation. A lot of which was conducted via intermediaries and unsung heroes operating on the fringes of the professional intelligence community for the common good. But it was also because Khrushchev held his nerve and backed away from a very dangerous game of hubris.

Could the world have gone to nuclear war in 1962? We will never know. Compared to the Soviet Union the United States had overwhelming and massive conventional and nuclear firepower, outnumbering the Warsaw Pact many times over. A US National Security Council report on the October 1962 Cuban Missile Crisis correctly judged that the Russians had at most 10 ICBMs at war readiness, a figure since endorsed by former Soviet scientists and military officers.

One of those was Oleg Penkovsky, the high-ranking GRU (military intelligence) operative who informed the West in 1962 of weaknesses with existing and planned Soviet missile programmes. The CIA sought the help of MI6 which recruited businessman Greville Wynn to be the intermediary, carrying messages to Penkovsky and returning with intelligence information.

What Penkovsky provided to Kennedy and to British premier Harold Macmillan was crucial to the way the Cuban Missile Crisis was handled at the White House and in Whitehall, London. Penkovsky was arrested in October 1962 and executed in Moscow on May 14, 1963.

Wynn was arrested in Moscow during October 1962, a month after the Cuba crisis and held in the KGB's Lubyanka prison but he was exchanged for the Russian spy known as Gordon Lonsdale in April 1964. Returning to London he died in February 1990.

ABOVE: An aerial reconnaissance shot of the San Cristobel site with removal of missiles underway by November 1. The crisis slowing dissipated as the Russians backed down in exchange for Jupiter missiles being removed from Italy and Turkey. (DIA)

CHAPTER NINE

CULTURE WARS

The world into which JFK became President was changing at a faster pace than at any other time within living memory. Despite two world wars, a depression, poverty, and a renewed boom in consumerism and prosperity in the 1950s, the 1960s brought a countercultural revolution with which prevailing norms of human behaviour, social attitudes and ethical mores were changing fast.

The availability of new forms of information connected people to the larger world across the United States, and out to the four corners of the globe where many Americans were serving at military bases and in allied countries under a NATO (North Atlantic Treaty Organisation) flag. Many had returned from World War Two having experienced the world outside America for the first time. Now some of those who had served, and their sons, were returning as the military presence increased, the alliance now more robustly consolidated after the Korean War of 1950-1953.

ABOVE: During the Kennedy years, anti-American feeling was strong in a wide range of countries. This sentiment stimulated a sense of cultural injustice in many US politicians eager to project a softer, kinder face to uncommitted countries. (Erik Cleves Kristensen)

ABOVE: 'New age' politicians such as the Kennedys used the universality of television to broadcast their message, Hollywood-style. (Author's collection)

The great tide of US military deployment for campaigns in World War Two had introduced a new culture to many countries, especially the UK where 1.5m Americans had been based, either supporting air raids on occupied Europe or transiting to battlefronts in North Africa, Italy and eventually the beaches of Normandy. The 'Americanisation' of British cultural life had been pervasive and for many irresistible as everything from food to movies and the broader range of social conventions went through a radical transformation affecting life everywhere.

Resistance to this cultural change was found in British comics for boys and girls with *Eagle*, *Swift* and *Robin* launched specifically to counter the influx of cheap paperbacks from America and proclaiming the preservation of 'British values' for British youth growing up in post-war Britain and the increasing secularisation of communities.

And the United States too was growing and changing at unprecedented speed, the population expanding from 148m in 1950 to 176m by 1960. In 1959, the admission of Alaska and Hawaii had raised the number of US states to 50, bringing new growth and an expansion of opportunity for their citizens. There was a profound feeling that this was the 'American Century', and that the USA was more engaged than ever, having thrown away its isolationist policies that had dominated political debate in the 1930s until the US naval base of Pearl Harbor on the Hawaiian island of Oahu had been attacked by Japan on December 7, 1941.

A NEW MEDIA

For a few, the world was exciting but to the majority the ability to receive entertainment in their own homes was an unimaginable indulgence. The advent of radio in the 1920s had revolutionised how politicians could speak to the nation, reaching several million people at the same time. What they said mattered because their voices could be heard, perhaps for

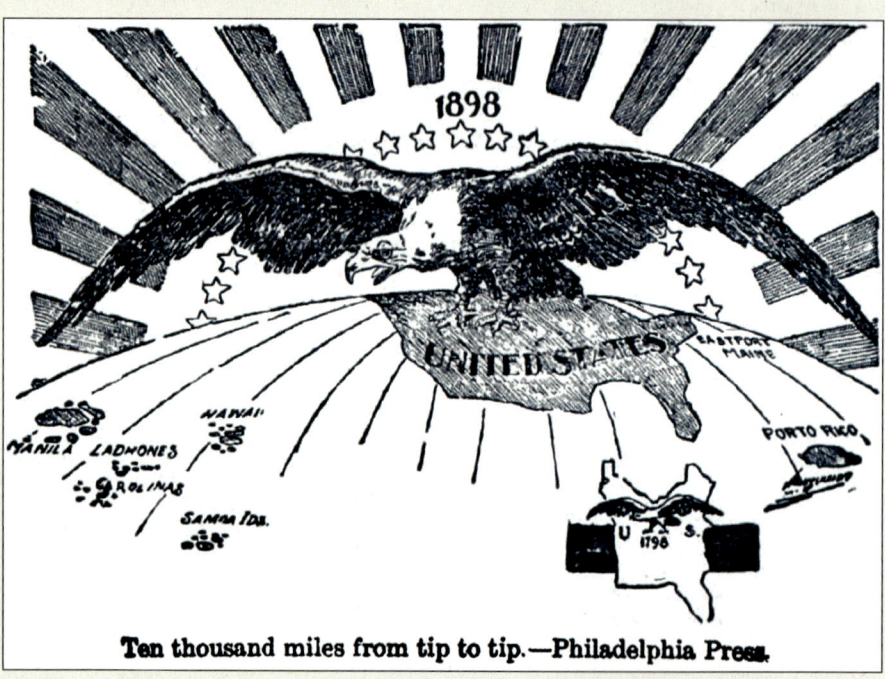

ABOVE: In a surprising inversion to what many Americans had believed, the strong notion of Pax Americana stretching from the Atlantic Ocean to the Philippines began to attract anti-cultural revolt against the 'old' order establishment during the early 1960s. (Philadelphia Press)

88 JFK – A LIFE REMEMBERED

CULTURE

the first time and that was a revolution in itself. President Franklin D Roosevelt had made great use of radio for his 'fireside chats' and international correspondents used the medium to bring reports to Americans in their homes and to tell Americans about life abroad, an obsession with British life being evident on US TV channels.

And then came moving pictures in the home. In 1950 television reached into 4.4m households, a mere 11% of the total number. By 1960 ten times that number had TV sets, a staggering 88%. And no longer was it voices that dominated, it was how the people appeared, a transformation in what the voters noticed. No longer their words alone but now their physical features, the undisguised way they looked on screen, even how they perspired under difficult questioning. All of which had seen Nixon fall dramatically to Kennedy in the polls during their own televised debates.

The profligate advance of consumerism fuelled the new world of TV shows, entertainment, and advertising. Unlike the UK where national public broadcasting dominated, in America a new industry arose for selling wares, encouraging local advertising from the corner store to the town realtor and supporting the intrusive marketing of new cars. Graphic news pictures drove home grim realities about the wider world and the government got in on the act with its public information broadcasts and a new youth culture emerged.

Some of that resonated with disturbing undertones. During the Eisenhower administration a public information campaign was launched with instructions on how families could protect themselves against the effects of an atomic bomb. Known as 'Duck and Cover', it was a flawed attempt to quell fears but only incited more concern in many people for whom the atom bomb had only been an event at the end of the war to bring Imperial Japan to its knees. Driven home by a public information campaign, the reality of a potential Soviet threat played no small part in a peace movement supported by students and musicians and several Hollywood film producers.

In ways they had never exerted influence before, campus campaigns and protests against war, the 'establishment' and constraints on personal freedom were hailed by activists as a slight on their constitutional rights. The youth saw these transformations and wanted a clearer role in deciding their own future, a more assertive intervention in the major decisions of the day, choosing protest as a mechanism for change. The Kennedy years in the White House were brief in time but seismic in sowing the seeds of cultural change and the emergence of the counter-culture movement.

Now, the young had access to youth movements and that became a key component in a wave of idealised disillusionment about the consumer-led society and the lack of balance between rich and poor. For a new generation born after the war, the 1960s were troubled times

ABOVE: Senator Joseph McCarthy used his position as a fightback from liberal thinking, seeking to use public office to make support for radical political doctrine, especially communism, illegal. (NARA)

ABOVE: Rejecting constraints many in the youth culture believed were imposed by the 'establishment', young people in the 1960s used popular music to seek an expression silenced in other creative arts. (Author's collection)

ABOVE: An early convert to human rights, Jack Kennedy worked with Eleanor Roosevelt, widow of the former President Franklin D Roosevelt, to engage with the Presidential Commission on the Status of Women. (NARA)

ABOVE: Responding to the perception that 'Americanism' was a corrosive influence on national culture, in small countries around the world radical and revolutionary leaders such as Che Guevara (left) and Fidel Castro mobilised bands of support. (NARA)

ABOVE: Opposing intervention where insurgents in foreign countries threatened totalitarian control, American youth rose up against what was perceived to be a new form of colonialism contrary to their liberal and free-thinking views. The creeping involvement of US 'advisers' in Southeast Asia was just one of these unwelcome phenomena. (UA Army Signal Corps)

CHAPTER NINE

ABOVE: As part of his New Frontier programme, on June 10, 1963 President Kennedy signed into law the equal pay act giving women the same wage as men for doing the same job. (Abbie Rowe/JFK Library)

when threats of atomic warfare and fanatical communists drove dissent and hatred. But the establishment of traditionalists in high positions of power sought to discredit radical protagonists of change. That in itself fuelled action at the top of government to root out 'Un-American activities' which hit celebrities, Hollywood actors, even leading writers and opinion-shapers of the day exhibiting the slightest whiff of socialism.

The so-called McCarthy 'witch-hunts' of the 1940s and 1950s when President Truman passed a law requiring all civil service employees be screened for communist leanings ran their course until public disaffection with such draconian restrictions on liberal speech and free thought brought about its demise. The legacy of these 'trials' of public loyalty helped stimulate anti-establishment fervour during the later 1950s and the 1960s.

EXPRESSIONS OF CHOICE

Profoundly significant to a new countercultural wave of protest and rejection, of the establishment and the status-quo, was the music that new radio and TV channels provided. By 1960 the influence of television on music and pop culture was driven by the fascination people had with the new media. Surveys showed that in mid-1960 the average American spent four to five hours each day watching the small screen, with the new dimension that had exploded into American homes becoming as significant in daily life as schools and churches had been to people a decade before.

Access to that and a seemingly unconstrained use of electronic media appeared to satisfy audiences across the country, but the shaping of the American mind through television was held by three commercial network offices in Manhattan, New York. Operated by the Federal Communications Commission (FCC), they invoked the universal 'freedom of the press' to restrain from controls on content or the vetting of contentious programmes. It was in essence a license for a free media and American culture was launched around the world by US TV shows and by endless TV Westerns crafting an image of the United States that the producers wanted to create.

Considered balanced, according to historian Theodore White, between "breath-taking magnificence and a squalid expression of American culture," television got the attention of the political elite, worried about the lack of interest in voter registration. In 1960, of the 107m Americans of qualified age, 40m had not bothered to register and that brought the media companies on a national drive to whip up enthusiasm for what many people considered a pointless exercise. Over time, however, the integration of public information schemes and a greater enthusiasm for participation in national decisions raised the registration levels.

Society was becoming more open in discussions, overturning previously constrained debate on sensitive matters and personal choices. The 1960s saw the beginning of an acceptance of different sexual choices, about the liberated acceptance of lesbian and gay people and about ideas of

ABOVE: One among many victims of racial abuse during the early 1960s, Malcolm X would lose his life to extremists from a radical movement. (Ed Ford/Library of Congress)

ABOVE: Martin Luther King was among several black leaders who marched on Washington on August 28, 1963 to stand at the Lincoln Memorial and protest against racial discrimination. (NARA)

90 JFK – A LIFE REMEMBERED

CULTURE

ABOVE: So called Yippies and protest movements began to infiltrate universities, recruiting supporters and frequently holding campaigns in a culture/counterculture revolution. (NARA)

ABOVE: Renewal of an idea of US exceptionalism took off in the early 1960s with beautification of American urban expansion and the magnificence of a new architectural style, epitomised here by the original McMillan plan for Washington DC. (Carol M Highsmith)

'recreational sex'. A revolution of the age and one which was liberally explored in art, drama, film, and TV. Crafted so as to provide an exploration of prohibited behaviour, the Kennedy years involuntarily pioneered transformative and accepted standards which are today taken as conventional norms.

Lifestyle changes helped this along, given momentum by science when the Food and Drug Administration legalised use of the Enovid contraceptive pill from 1960. Within two years, 1.2m American women were taking 'the pill'. By 1965, a quarter of all married women under 45 were regular users but that brought down the number of children per family. However, immigrants from abroad seeking a better life in the United States grew the population beyond 200m in 1969 for the first time. More adults but fewer children, starting a downward trend falling from 2.33 in 1960 to 0.78 in 2022.

CIVIL RIGHTS

Of profound significance to many Americans, the civil rights movement which flowered in the 1960s grew out of repressive and cruel exclusions on the lives of black people left hanging by legislation dating back to the mid-19th century and unresolved issues from the American Civil War of 1861-1865. Combating the punitive laws in some southern states, the Civil Rights Act of 1957 signed by Eisenhower prohibited the exclusion of any US citizen from voting. It abolished literacy tests on blacks and coloured people, opening the way to universal rights.

In 1960 four black college students refused to leave a Woolworth's lunch counter where they were refused service because of their colour, attracting several hundred supporting their rights as American citizens. This single event stimulated a campus-wide campaign for the civil rights movement and a long, hard struggle for equality under the law. During the 1950s prejudice had been rife as vigilantes formed mobs to oppose free access to areas designated for white people, including transport.

In May 1961 'freedom riders' began a coach tour protesting against segregation on the buses, but violence broke out, firebombs were thrown, and many were badly beaten by a mob of whites. Unable to find a driver to take them on another bus, Robert Kennedy stepped in and negotiated a replacement but further on they were arrested in Jacksonville, Mississippi for trespassing on a 'whites-only' facility and jailed for 30 days. Pressure from the Kennedy administration brought about new regulations prohibiting segregation.

Over the next two years the movement grew and on August 28, 1963, a march on Washington brought 200,000 people to hear Martin Luther King appeal for universal rights for all as he made his now famous "I have a dream…" speech. Born in 1929, King became the de facto leader of the civil rights movement with his passive, non-violent appeal for basic human respect, with equality under law and decency for all.

King's inspiration ran far and wide around the world and his assassination on April 4, 1968 shocked most Americans and immortalised his memory. Two months later, for very different reasons Robert Kennedy too had been assassinated. The 1960s were ending but the die had been cast. Changes had liberated many Americans and founded a countercultural revolution which would reappear under different labels in the following years. But what had begun in that decade would for ever be viewed as a foundation stone for changes that could only have been imagined a few years earlier.

ABOVE: Fashion become key to how many young people came to see themselves in the early 1960s, new trends made affordable in post-war economic growth. (Joan Atherton)

ABOVE: Freedom of expression in life and among the new youth culture attracted new ways of education, including the 'free-school' concept devoid of strict curricula and formal class structures. (Axel Kuhn)

CHAPTER TEN

FEUDING FAMILIES

It may not be the image the general public gets to see very often, but playing a second-best role in politics can lead to bitter clashes, usually behind the gaze of the voter and always with the intention of bettering personal chances and new opportunities. When a giant in congressional circles, a self-made achiever and a larger-than-life character with a big ego and a desire for greatness is thwarted by a young and relatively inexperienced newcomer, sparks will fly.

So it was when Jack Kennedy received the nomination of the Democratic Party in 1960 to stand for President at that year's November election. Lyndon Baines Johnson (LBJ) believed he had the right to that position and would never forget that he had failed to be the nominee of choice from a party he had worked for all his life. Climbing over the bodies of the subdued and with an enormous talent for manipulating people and for bribing loyalty in exchange for political support, Johnson would never go quietly into the night.

Born on August 27, 1908 in a farmhouse on the outskirts of Stonewall, Texas, Johnson's father was a high school teacher and Lyndon himself the eldest of five children including three girls. The family had descended from Irish, German, and Scottish ancestry and LBJ was the great-grandson of the pioneering Baptist preacher George Washington Baines on his mother's side. Perhaps because of their background, the family had a tolerant attitude to religious affiliations and was intolerant of anti-Semitism which was prevalent at the time in some States.

ABOVE: Following naval service during World War Two, Johnson returned to politics that had been his passion since school days. (USN)

Even by the standards of the time, the family was poor. The house had no electricity and the 'dirt farm' existence instilled in LBJ a profound sense of injustice in the way the lower levels of society were left to fend for themselves, welfare and benefits being virtually non-existent. Angered by the products of destitution, mobilised by a desire to change things, the talkative young Lyndon made his views known during public speaking events at his school and later in college.

Coming from an unaccredited school his father pressed for him to go to college but at 16 he left home temporarily and went to California where he worked at his cousin's legal practice while doing odd manual jobs including rock-breaking for new roads in the area. Installed at a college affiliated to the Southwest Texas State Teachers College (now Texas State University) at the age of 18, Lyndon edited the school paper, engaged in debate, and got involved in campus politics. Working his own way through college, he finished his education in 1930 with a BSc in history and politics and secured a position teaching public speaking at Sam Houston High School in Houston.

Motivated by his experiences while tutoring Mexican-American children, he would recall later: "I shall never forget the faces of the boys and the girls in that little Welhausen Mexican School, and I remember even yet the pain of realizing and knowing then that college was closed to practically every one of those children because they

ABOVE: As Vice President, Lyndon B Johnson was denied the powers he once held in the Senate and that rankled, influencing his relationship with Jack Kennedy, and creating rift. (Author's collection)

92 JFK – A LIFE REMEMBERED

FAMILY TROUBLES

ABOVE: Kennedy and Johnson struggled to present a unified front, a disparity which in reality was contrary to their similar views in the liberal wing of the Democratic Party. (NARA)

were too poor. And I think it was then that I made up my mind that this nation could never rest while the door to knowledge remained closed to any American."

Working his way into politics, he served in the House of Representatives from 1937 to 1949 and everywhere he spoke, people listened. From 1941 to 1945 he served with the US Navy and fought for better conditions in the Pacific theatre, using a movie film he made to impress upon President Roosevelt the need for better supplies and equipment for military campaigns, a message which did little to endear him to senior officers struggling with minimal resources as American struggled on multiple fronts.

After the war, Johnson ran for the Senate and won in the 1948 election, climbing rapidly through the maze of Washington politics to become the Democratic Party whip. When the Republican Party won a majority in the House and the Senate in 1952, Johnson was made Democratic Minority Leader, setting his sights on the nomination for President at the 1960 election, but he was handicapped by a late entry.

Faced with a coordinated and well-funded campaign from Jack Kennedy, already a formidable contender bringing charm and intelligence to the bid, Johnson challenged the younger man on his health issues and on his youth and inexperience. But popularity among the party traditionalists and support from many in the Democratic Party failed to win the day and Kennedy was selected by 806 votes to Johnson's 409. Johnson was selected for the Kennedy ticket because he could bring the much needed southern states to the presidential campaign and not because there was very much they shared, either in background or political ideals.

THE 'LITTLE RUNT'

From the time of the decision to put LBJ on the ticket, Robert Kennedy got the brunt of the opinionated and strident Johnson, who described Jack as a "scrawny little fellow with rickets," referring to Jack's Addison's disease and his regular doses of cortisone. But the Kennedys never responded in kind. LBJ had recovered from a heart attack in 1955 but outspoken and public vitriol would do nothing to get either man in power, so the bitterness was constrained, albeit extending out into their families with only whispered reference to Johnson's own health.

During the contest for nomination as party nominee, Lyndon Johnson was, however, quite vocal about the Catholic vote sought by the Kennedy family – his father

ABOVE: Lyndon Jonson is sworn in as President on November 22, 1963 aboard *Air Force One* on the flight back from Dallas, Texas. (NARA)

still exceptionally active with his money and political influence and intent on recruiting that group. But Johnson was aware that some of the Kennedy family manipulated events using unsavoury figures associated with crime gangs and union bosses and he chafed at that. Especially at the coterie of Hollywood stars and the 'rat pack' recruited for bringing on the crowds, mixing entertainment with political campaigning.

For a while before the presidential election, Robert Kennedy sensed real trouble ahead, with the Republican Party likely to exploit heated differences between the two as the debates began to take on a serious undertone. Robert Kennedy was pressed by northern states to get Johnson off the ticket and reverse the decision of the party. Robert was unsuccessful, earning him Johnson's enmity as the "grandstanding little runt." But the distaste for each other spilled over to their respective wives and while Johnson's wife Lady Bird was sanguine about the whole

BELOW: The Kennedy family home at Hyannis Port, a veritable compound with typical architecture of the windswept coastline. (Interstellarity/wiki commons)

> "By the end of 1968, the three eldest Kennedy boys were dead, and the Johnson presidency was over, succeeded by the Nixon era at the ballot box."

www.keymilitary.com 93

CHAPTER TEN

ABOVE: The Kennedy family gather at Hyannis Port on September 4, 1931 with (from left) Robert F, John F, Eunice, Jean (on lap) of Joseph P Snr, Rose (pregnant with Edward), Patricia, Kathleen, Joseph Jnr (behind) and Rosemary.
(Richard Sears/JFK Library)

the time such divisions were largely because of fierce and competitive jousts. Johnson failed to understand the attraction for Jack Kennedy and for the 'boys from Boston' who were able to overthrow traditional lines of political accession and beat the bookies to the White House, where, until those TV debates, Richard Nixon had been favourite.

Johnson saw the vice presidency as a poisoned chalice, claiming that "every time I came into John Kennedy's presence, I felt like a goddam raven hovering over his shoulder." And there are many who felt that Bobby Kennedy stood for the presidential election in 1964 because he could not bear to think that Johnson would inherit his brother's desk in the Oval Office. Added to which, Bobby never forgave Johnson for having played so large a part in bringing Jack to Dallas on the day he was killed.

A FAMILY AFFAIR

By the end of 1968, the three eldest Kennedy boys were dead, and the Johnson presidency was over, succeeded by the Nixon era at the ballot box on November 5 and at

relationship, Jackie Kennedy had a deep-seated dislike for the Texan.

Born on December 22, 1912 in Karnack, Texas, Claudia Alta 'Lady Bird' Johnson (nee Taylor) was brought up in wealth and position, her family owning 6,070 hectares (15,000 acres) of cotton as well as two general stores. Possessing considerable intelligence, she graduated from the University of Texas with degrees in history and journalism. Introduced to Lyndon Johnson by a friend, they were married on November 17, 1934. The marriage was strained by Lyndon's numerous and long lasting affairs, and she would later say how she felt "humiliated" by his frequent boasts to having had more sexual encounters with women than the President. This continued throughout his own presidency, which lasted from November 1963 to January 1969.

After the election of November 1960, the acrimonious exchanges got worse when Johnson let it be known that he alone had secured the narrow victory by bringing along the southern votes. To British readers much of this may appear due to a sense of Johnson's class inferiority but in reality, in America at

ABOVE: JFK with Carolyn when she was five years old. (NARA)

ABOVE: John Junior gets a personal tour of the White House grounds by the President himself. (NARA)

94 JFK – A LIFE REMEMBERED

the swearing in on January 20, 1969. But there was another Kennedy in the political world of the nation's capital, ably capable of supporting the family name.

Born on February 22, 1932, Edward 'Ted' Kennedy was sworn in to the Senate on November 7, 1962 during the immediate aftermath of the Cuban Missile Crisis. His politics were largely those of his two elder brothers and he brought the acclaimed family name and law degrees to the job. But on June 19, 1964 he had a brush with death and only just survived a plane crash when his private Aero Commander 680 came down in poor weather, the wreckage from which he was pulled by fellow Senator Birch Bayer, incurring an enduring chronic back pain for the rest of his life.

On the night of July 18, 1969 after leaving a late party he had held for the Boiler Room Girls, a group of women who had supported Robert's presidential campaign, at Chappaquiddick Island at the eastern end of Martha's Vineyard, Ted Kennedy was driving across a bridge. He lost control of the car which plunged into the waters of the Poucha Pond inlet, trapping his passenger, Mary Jo Kopechne. He swam to shore leaving her to drown and fled the scene. For leaving the scene of an accident he was given a two-year suspended prison sentence.

Ted Kennedy was re-elected to the Senate in November 1970, becoming outspoken on The Troubles in Northern Ireland, asserting that it was "Britain's Vietnam." For the rest of his life Ted Kennedy fought for the principles of the Democratic Party although the event at Chappaquiddick haunted him and tarnished his reputation. Diagnosed with brain cancer he succumbed on August 25, 2009.

Ted's nephew Joseph P Kennedy II and his son Patrick J served in the House of Representatives. In 2012 Joseph P Kennedy III, the grandson of Robert Kennedy, won a seat in the House and is currently the US Special Envoy for Northern Ireland. At present, two

ABOVE: Edward Kennedy carried the family name to great heights during his long and distinguished career, flawed by an incident in which he fled a car accident in which his passenger died. (JFK Library)

other Kennedys are serving the government: Victoria Reggie, second wife of Edward is the ambassador to Austria, and Caroline, daughter of JFK is now the ambassador to Japan.

Joseph P Kennedy Sr and his wife Rose lived through the tragic and untimely deaths of their three elder sons, but Joseph died on November 18, 1969 while Rose passed away on January 22, 1995 at the age of 104 years. Birth and death dates of all their children are listed in the chronology at the back of this book.

The only son who came close to following JFK into the top job at the White House was Robert Kennedy, of whom perhaps too little is said. In mourning the loss of his elder brother in June 1968, Edward Kennedy expressed what many believed to be true about the man who came so close and was denied his rightful seat through the senseless actions of an assassin:

"My brother need not be idealized, or enlarged in death beyond what he was in life; to be remembered simply as a good and decent man, who saw wrong and tried to right it, saw suffering, and tried to heal it, saw war, and tried to stop it. Those of us who loved him and who take him to his rest today, pray that what he was to us and what he wished for others will someday come to pass for all the world. As he said many times, in many parts of this nation, to those he touched and who sought to touch him: 'Some men see things as they are and say why? I dream things that never were and say why not'?"

ABOVE: A prominent socialite during her life, Patricia Kennedy married Peter Lawford in 1954 but they divorced in 1966 and she died of pneumonia in 2006. (JFK Library)

ABOVE: An ambassador to Australia since 2022, Carolyn Kennedy has achieved several careers in one lifetime, also being an author, attorney, and diplomat. (US Department of State)

CHAPTER ELEVEN

THE ASSASSINATION

The final year of President Kennedy's life was spent recovering from the crises over Berlin and Cuba and to beginning the process of seeing through legislation for the New Frontier programme that had been unsuccessful in changing die-hard and conservative politicians. Particularly in the south of the country where traditionalist feelings ran high and held sway.

There was much work to be done, with the presidential election in November 1964 and preparations for a campaign to get JFK re-elected to the White House. It had not been an easy ride, little more than a thousand days so far in trying to change America and make the real and positive difference to which both Jack and Robert were committed.

There was discord in the southern state of Texas which needed resolving, raising support, and smoothing frictions between the liberal Democratic Party Senator Ralph Yarborough and the conservative Governor John Connolly. A visit had been agreed in June during a meeting in El Paso, Texas where party bosses got together to effect change.

Texans are not known for their liberal ways, and challenges of bringing what were considered by many to be such policies brought problems for the administration. And the rift was great, Yarborough and Connolly refusing to ride together in a motorcade planned for the visit to Dallas on November 22, 1963. Lyndon Johnson was to be along, always providing support for the party in his home state and cracking heads together for the good of the party.

Air Force One touched down at Carswell Air Force Base, Texas, at 11.07pm on November 21 and the President and his wife arrived at the Hotel Texas in Fort Worth 28 minutes later having been cheered on their way by crowds packed along the West Freeway, pausing on arrival to linger with well-wishers before retiring to their suite, Room 850. *Air Force Two* had landed at Carswell carrying Vice President Johnson and his wife, Texas Governor John Connolly, and Senator Ralph Yarborough.

The following morning at 8:45am, Jack gave a short speech before breakfast, praising the

BELOW: The Kennedy's arrive at Dallas on the bright and clear morning of November 22, 1963 with a planned motorcade, a recruiting campaign for Democratic Party support. (NARA)

ABOVE: Lee Harvey Oswald when he was in the US Marine Corps. (USMC)

aerospace accomplishments of the state and singling out Fort Worth for its aviation industry dominated in the area by Lockheed. Carefully crafted words were needed in this Republican-dominated town. Against the preferences of the Secret Service and in view of the clement weather, Kenneth O'Donnell radioed ahead to Dallas to say that the motorcade could give the President and his wife an open-top ride.

> "The following morning at 8:45am, Jack gave a short speech before breakfast, praising the aerospace accomplishments of the state and singling out Fort Worth for its aviation industry dominated in the area by Lockheed."

After a short flight covering the 55km (35 miles) from Carswell to Love Field, Dallas, the dignitaries arrived at 11:38am to be met by the motorcade to take them from the airport to the Trade Mart, arriving at 12:15pm where the President was to deliver a short speech before enjoying a steak lunch. The procession from Love Field was delayed about 15 minutes as the Kennedy's paused to engage with onlookers.

Fourteen cars and two press buses were lined up as the motorcade began its winding journey through Dallas. But someone else was in Dallas that day, a man who would be propelled through his actions to an infamous chapter in the history of the United States. A name that would soon be known around the world.

BIOGRAPHY OF AN ASSASSIN

Born in New Orleans, Louisiana, on October 18, 1939, Lee Harvey Oswald was related to two great names in US history. His father Robert was the third cousin of President Theodore Roosevelt and distantly related to the Confederate General Robert E Lee, after whom his son was named. Robert and his wife Marguerite had married in 1933 and their first son John was born in 1934. Robert died of a heart attack in August 1939 just two months before Lee, their second son was born.

Marguerite moved herself and the two boys to Dallas, Texas in 1944 when Lee was five years old where he started grade school in the Fort Worth area. Marguerite married Edwin Ekdahl later that year, but they separated in 1946 and divorced in 1948, when she formally changed her name to Marguerite Oswald. Four years later Marguerite moved to New York with Lee and for a while she and her second son lived with John and his 18-year old wife Marge who had a three-month old son. The women failed to get along and life became turbulent in an increasingly dysfunctional household.

When Lee enrolled in a junior high school in the Bronx he was bullied and set upon due to his Texas accent and style of clothing. The older brother saw a marked change in Lee as he became more contemptuous of authority, disrespectful to the family and after pulling a knife on Marge in a threatening move he left the home along with his mother to a single basement room and Marguerite started work at Lerner Shops, a women's workwear outlet. When truancy charges were brought against Lee for non-attendance at school, he was sent to a Youth House where he was subject to psychological analysis for three weeks from mid-April 1953.

The prognosis from Dr Renatus Hartogs determined that Lee was a "quite disturbed youngster who suffers under the impact of really existing emotional isolation and deprivation, lack of affection, absence of family life and rejection by a self-involved and conflicted mother." It was recommended that Lee receive psychiatric treatment in a child guidance clinic and a social worker, Evelyn D Siegel wrote that there was "a rather pleasant, appealing quality about this emotionally starved, affectionless youngster which grows as one speaks to him," judging the reason for his behaviour to be that no one "ever met any of his needs for love."

There was little improvement in Lee's behaviour until a transformation brought about when he was threatened with being moved to a boys' home. With the case still open and a final decision pending, in January 1954 mother and son moved back to New Orleans where Lee completed his mandatory education before working at odd jobs for a year. While there he joined

> "Someone else was in Dallas that day, a man who would be propelled through his actions to an infamous chapter in the history of the United States."

CHAPTER ELEVEN

BELOW: The Minsk apartment block where Lee Harvey Oswald briefly lived. (Jerrye and Roy Klotz)

the Civil Air Patrol (CAP), an officially sanctioned voluntary organisation for air-minded enthusiasts, and in October 1956 he joined the Marines. In his 17 years he had attended 12 schools and lived in 22 places.

An avid reader, despite being diagnosed with a 'reading-spelling' disorder, he was drawn to socialism and communism which, according to his diary, came to him as he dug through the 'back dusty shelves of libraries'. Contacting the Socialist Party of America, he found access to organisations of similar mind but failed to impress diehard socialists that he was a 'true believer', judged by his close friend Edward Voerbel to be merely the willing recipient of 'paperback trash'.

Provided with low-level security clearance, Lee Oswald was assigned to radar operations and did well at Keesler Air Force Base in Mississippi where he was given classification as an electronic operator. Assigned to a naval air squadron near Tokyo, Japan, he learned to shoot, getting a grade slightly above 'sharpshooter'. Lee Oswald was court-martialled twice, the first time for accidentally shooting himself in the arm and then for fighting with the sergeant he believed to have been responsible for that trial.

There then began a strange period in which he appeared obsessed with Soviet Russia and, intent on making dramatic changes to his life, carving out an entirely different future based on a proclaimed conversion to the communist world in a more direct and intense way than in any of his previous dealings with political ideology.

Oswald began to learn Russian, but on February 25, 1959 scored poorly in a Marine proficiency test on spoken word while achieving higher ratings for reading and writing. In September 1959 he received a hardship discharge, claiming that his mother needed special care and he went on the reserve list.

With $1,500 in saved pay, the following month, just before his 20th birthday he left the country for Le Havre by ship. From there he went to Southampton on the south coast of England, arriving on October 9 and immediately flying to Helsinki, Finland. There, he got a seven-day visa to Russia and travelled to Moscow by train, arriving on October 16 before mandatorily checking in with an Intourist guide.

Oswald immediately declared his desire to become a Russian citizen but when asked why his answers were evasive and indistinct. He would not be allowed to stay. Reacting to the news, in an attempt to impress his guide with his convictions he cut his wrist

ASSASSINATION

> "Despite harbouring high ideas of attending Moscow University, Oswald was sent to an electronics factory in Belarus."

in the hotel bathtub. He was sent to the psychiatric ward of a local hospital, visits by several Soviet officials resulting in further questioning where he declared his service with the Marines. On October 31 he visited the US Embassy and declared that he wanted to defect and blatantly admitted that he wanted to share secrets with his new country.

Oswald was given a discharge on grounds of mental instability and the Russian authorities reversed their decision when he offered to tell them all he knew about the Marine Corps. Despite harbouring high ideas of attending Moscow University, Oswald was sent to an electronics factory in Belarus where he befriended Stanislaus Shushkevich, who would become the first head of the independent Belarusian state after the collapse of the Soviet Union. It was he who helped Oswald with his conversational Russian while Oswald struck up a relationship with Ella German with whom he worked. Their relationship ended when she discovered that Oswald had been unfaithful.

It was in January 1961, when the United States was celebrating the inauguration of JFK as the 35th US President that Oswald began to confide to his diary that he was "starting to reconsider my desire about staying," complaining that "the work is drab" and that "the money I get has nowhere to be spent." In fact, he had been set up in a pleasant apartment with good pay and a special supplement for having provided an embarrassment to the US government. In America, the news broke that a serviceman had defected, drawing considerable attention from the press.

It transpired that the paperwork for rejecting US citizenship had never been completed and he wrote to the US Embassy in Moscow asking for his passport back and for any charges against him be dropped if they would please allow him back in to America. At this time, he married Marina Prusakova and their first child, June was born on February 15, 1962 before papers came through for his return, together with a loan of $453.71 to give them a start back in the United States.

On his return Oswald was disappointed at the apparent lack of interest in him from the press but he settled in the Dallas/Fort Worth area not far from where his mother and elder brother lived. Through Marina, Oswald became acquainted with Russian emigres and while they engaged with her, they found him arrogant and self-centred, quickly drifting away from their company after she declared her intention to remain with him. Meanwhile, Oswald found employment as a sheet metal worker in Dallas but left after three months, joining a graphic art company as a trainee photo printer where he frequently got into fights.

Obsessed with guns, in March 1963, a month before he was sacked Oswald had bought a Smith & Wesson .38 revolver and a Mannlicher-Carcano rifle from a mail order catalogue under an alias and with forged certificates. Friends among emigres testified to Oswald's fluency in Russian conversation and contrasted his erratic and abrasive attitude with his desire for reading and study which frequently worked to demean him in the company of others. Very few would ever say that they were close friends or that they really understood him.

There was an unsubstantiated accusation that Oswald had taken a pot-shot at General Edwin Anderson Walker, an anti-communist agitator and ardent segregationist who Oswald regarded as a fascist and who had been discharged from the army after distributing extremist leaflets. Marina claimed that Oswald had taken a bus to his house and shot at him, but Walker refused to alert police and the event was only traced through a note Oswald left for his wife instructing her on what to do if he failed to return.

Oswald returned to New Orleans on April 24 and Marina joined him a month later when he got a job greasing coffee machines in a local shop, but he was fired for spending all his time in an adjacent garage reading hunting magazines. The following month Oswald contacted the Fair Play for Cuba organisation campaigning for Castro and offered to form a branch in New Orleans. Before hearing from them he ordered stationery, membership application forms and leaflets campaigning for 'Hands off Cuba'. Street campaigns brought Oswald into confrontation with an anti-Castro group, but it became clear that he had never been sanctioned by the group he professed to represent.

Marina left New Orleans for a friend's house in Irving, Texas and Oswald left in late

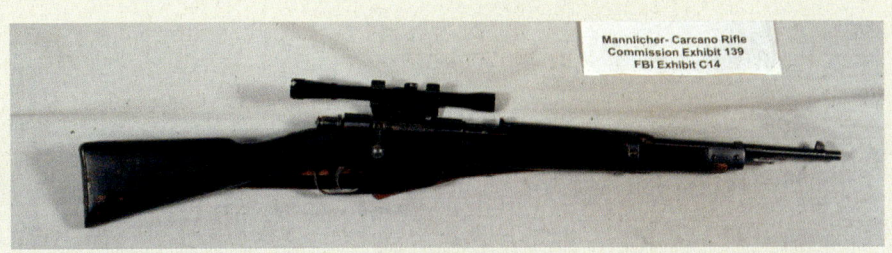

ABOVE: Lee Harvey Oswald married Marina who left Russia for a life in the United States and introduced him to Belarusian friends who found him coarse and disrespectful. (NARA)

ABOVE: The Mannlicher-Carcano rifle owned by Lee Harvey Oswald and the gun allegedly used to assassinate JFK. (US Justice Department)

CHAPTER ELEVEN

September with an unemployment cheque and, according to bus passengers, the stated aim of going to Cuba via Mexico. He got to Mexico City on September 27 and tried for a transit visa but was told he would need approval from the Russian Embassy to make the journey.

Over a series of several days, Oswald spoke unsuccessfully to KGB agents in Mexico, consular officials, and was shadowed by the CIA who had for long considered him to be a 'person of interest'. It is not known precisely what Oswald's plans were, an investigation as recently as 2017 indicated that he may have tried to set up an escape route back to Russia. However, there is speculation too about whether he ever went to Mexico, despite the main body of evidence substantiating that he did.

Whatever the intention, Oswald left Mexico City by bus on October 2 and was in Dallas the following day where he was told about a job going at the Texas School Book Depository for $1.25 an hour. He started there on October 16 and made a good impression, working hard and generally settling in well while renting a room under the name O H Lee. At weekends he would travel to Irving to see his wife, sharing a car ride with fellow employee Wesley Frazier. Four days after he started work there, Marina gave birth to her second daughter, Audrey.

Now back in the USA, Oswald came to the attentions of the FBI, his CIA file having been handed over after he departed Mexico. Twice agents visited his home without finding him in, after which Oswald left a note signed 'Lee Harvey Oswald' at the local FBI office: "Let this be a warning. I will blow up the FBI and the Dallas Police Department if you don't stop bothering my wife."

THREE SHOTS

Unusually, on Thursday November 21 Oswald asked Frazier for a lift to Irving where he wanted to collect a bag of curtain rods. They were back the next day, Oswald with his bag later determined to have contained

> "When truancy charges were brought against Lee for non-attendance at school, he was sent to a Youth House where he was subject to psychological analysis for three weeks."

BELOW: The house in Magazine St, New Orleans where Lee Harvey Oswald rented an apartment between May and September 1963. (Author's collection)

ASSASSINATION

his rifle. The day, November 22, that John F Kennedy took a motorcade through one of the most densely populated parts of the city for maximum visibility, riding against the advice of his security team in a 1961 Lincoln Continental convertible. They were on their way to the Dallas Market Center for a luncheon where Jack would give a speech.

The convoy had the Kennedy limousine second in the line of 14 cars threading their way through the crowd-lined thoroughfare. Jack and Jackie Kennedy sat in the back seats with Governor Connolly and his wife forward of them. In front was the driver, secret service agent Bill Greer with special agent Roy Kellerman alongside. The route that they followed from Love Field is no longer there. Certain roads have changed and only the main buildings, the primary freeways and some side roads remain.

The journey was uneventful, stopping twice for the Kennedys to shake hands with Catholic schoolchildren and nuns before proceeding along to Dealey Plaza, which it reached at 12:29pm local time. As it approached the Texas School Book Depository it made a sharp 135° turn into Elm St which was a slight incline sloping down toward the plaza and into a triple underpass. Governor Connolly's wife Nellie turned round, smiling: "Mr. President, they can't make you believe now that there are not some in Dallas who love and appreciate you, can they?" His reply were the last words he spoke: "No, they sure can't."

It was just 12:30pm when the first of three shots rang out with reports of second and third shots fired at close intervals. The first struck the President as he was waving to the crowds to his right and entered his upper back, exiting through his throat immediately below the larynx. It was an injury that he would probably have survived but a second shot was fired as the car reached the grassy knoll, the bullet striking the back of his head, taking fragments of flesh, bone and brain matter out and onto the secret service car immediately behind.

Agent Clint Hill leaped from the running board of the following car and recalled that about five seconds elapsed between the first and second shots and could be heard just as he reached the President's car, seeing Jackie throw herself over Jack's slumped body, blood everywhere. Connolly had himself been hit by the first bullet that struck the President and heard her exclaim "They have killed my husband. I have his brains in my hand." Connolly himself was injured but conscious, exclaiming "My God. They're going to kill us all."

Pandemonium broke out among the spectators, now aware that the motorcade was under attack. Several witnesses shouted that they were convinced second and third shots had come from the grassy knoll and police raced to check it out but could find nothing. Six minutes after the gunshots, teenager Amos Euins told police Sergeant D V Harkness that he had seen a man leaning out a window on the sixth floor of the book depository building and a search was quickly made, finding Oswald's rifle, later discovered to have his palm print on the butt. Another witness, Howard Brennan claimed he also saw the man while a third witness, William James R Worrall Jr verified that, and Bonnie Ray Williams claimed that the rifle shot from the floor above was sufficiently loud to bring plaster shavings down on his head.

The motorcade made a dash for the Parkland Hospital 7km (4 miles) away by the Stemmons Freeway and Harry Hines Boulevard, arriving at 12:35pm. Kennedy was pronounced dead at 1:00pm after the last rites had been read by Father Oscar Huber. Connolly received medical treatment at the same time, his injuries not fatal. Shortly thereafter procedures began to

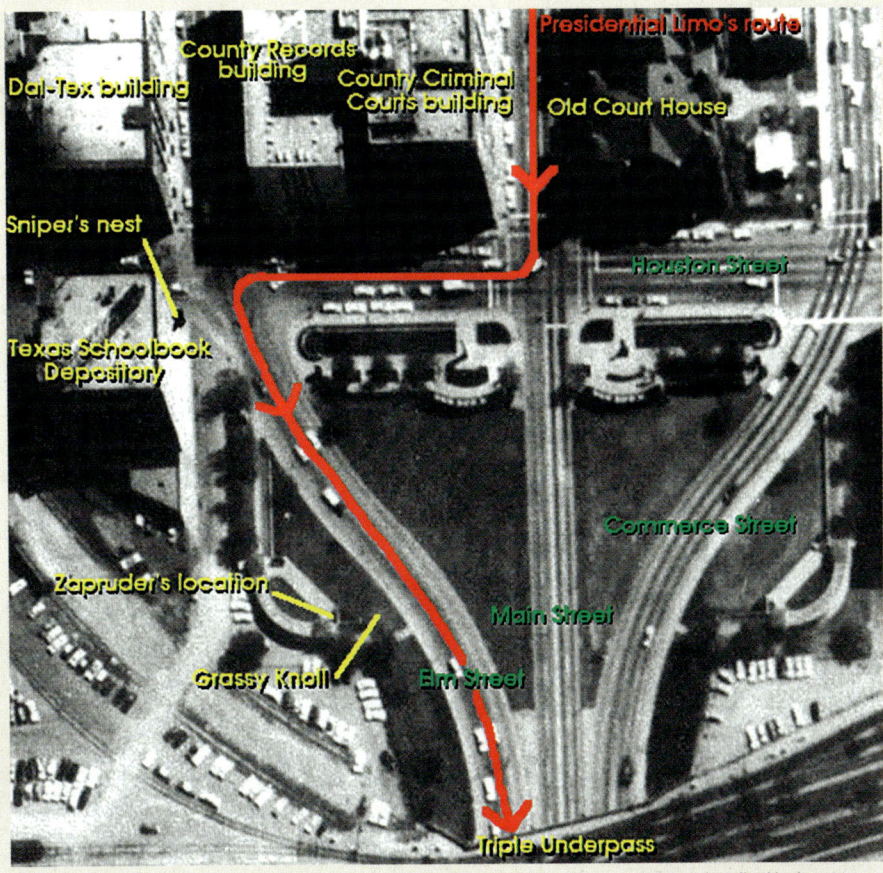

ABOVE: An annotated map of the motorcade route in Dallas showing key buildings and places described in the text. (Warren Commission)

CHAPTER ELEVEN

ABOVE: The motorcade provided a topless limousine for the ride through Dallas, with the President and Jackie in the rear seats, Governor Connolly, and his wife forward and behind the driver and secret service agent. (Warren Commission)

disperse the dignitaries from the motorcade for fear that it was a conspiracy to bring down the government.

A DOUBLE KILLING

Police officers had rushed to the Texas School Book Depositary building and met Oswald calmly leaving the building. Astonishingly, thought to be an employee, he was allowed to walk away and board a bus at 12:40pm. Stalled by intense traffic, Oswald asked to get off which he did before taking a taxi to his accommodation at North Beckley Avenue, going straight to his room. Minutes later he left with a zipper jacket he had collected and walked along, ostensibly to a bus stop. At about 1:15pm police officer J D Tippit spotted Oswald on the sidewalk and thought he looked like the man witnesses had described on the sixth floor of the Depositary.

Challenged by Tippit, Oswald shot him four times. As he lay dying, Oswald fled with numerous witnesses later identifying him as the attacker. Fleeing to a theatre he was followed by Johnny Brewer who alerted the police and Oswald was arrested but not before he pulled out his revolver, pointed it at Officer Nick McDonald and squeezed the trigger. It failed to fire when the hammer came down on the webbing of his jacket. With no place left to run to, Oswald was

taken to Dallas Police Headquarters and interrogated for two days. When asked during interview if he was a communist, he replied: "No, I am not a communist, I am a Marxist."

On November 24, police were escorting Oswald through the basement with

the intention of transporting him in an armoured car to the county jail, at 11:21am nightclub owner Jack Ruby stepped forward and shot him. Oswald died at 1:07pm and Ruby was sentenced to death but that was repealed, and he went to prison where he was diagnosed with cancer and died on

ABOVE: Less than a minute before the fatal shots, smiles from the limousine, its occupants unaware of the gunman, his target already in sight. (Warren Commission)

ASSASSINATION

January 3, 1967. Why had he killed Oswald? Because of his overwhelming grief over the assassination of Jack Kennedy, he said. Others continue to believe that he was paid to silence Oswald by Mafia bosses to prevent a court trial that could have revealed a greater conspiracy.

The body of Jack Kennedy lay in repose in the East Wing of the White House and November 23 was declared a national day of mourning. The funeral was held on November 25 at St Mathews Cathedral, attended by 1,200 guests and representatives from more than 90 countries. Excerpts from Kennedy's speeches and writings were read but there was no eulogy. He was buried at Arlington National Cemetery and an eternal flame was lit there in 1967. And so ended the 1,036 days of the Kennedy Presidency.

Events of great magnitude attract such theories and willing advocates with their own ideas. Readers can find these through web-based searches and in documentary films which continue to readdress events of 50 years ago. Some of that revision is credible, as new and successful ways of analysing evidence through scientific investigation becomes possible. Basic evidence, however, is prone to subjective interpretation and some of that dates right back to the day that these events took place.

Key to understanding the timeline and the sequence of events comes from the so-called Zapruder film, shot by Abraham Zapruder using an 8-mm Bell & Howell Zoomatic Model 414 camera that he had bought in 1962. Along with his secretary Marilyn Sitzman, Zapruder positioned himself on the grassy knoll north of Elm St in Dealey Plaza and shot 26.6 seconds of film on 486 frames of Kodak Kodachrome film, right at the time the shots rang out. The Zapruder film has been used variously to both verify and contradict the official version of events and continues to be used to challenge the conclusions of the official inquiry.

The official investigation was chaired by Chief Justice Earl Warren and reported its findings on September 24, 1964. Known as the Warren Commission, its conclusion was that Oswald alone fired the shots that killed Jack Kennedy and nobody else was involved, that there was no conspiracy involving other parties and that there was no participation by foreign powers. But it has not rested there and over time many challenges to the formal explanation have been made, some by official parties.

Numerous conspiracy theories have been put forward to suggest that there was more than one shooter, and evidence has been produced to indicate that there were groups wanting to bring down the Kennedy administration for reasons which have been identified in various preceding chapters of this book.

Some uncontested mystery surrounded the autopsy, where Jack's brain went missing from the National Archives where it had been preserved for scientific analysis while the medical report itself is acknowledged to be full of inconsistencies. Historians are generally agreed that the entire medical examination of the President's head was flawed, conducted by two doctors who were said to be insufficiently qualified for the work.

Defined as one of the finest rhetorical addresses he ever made, the words spoken by Jack Kennedy at the American University in Washington, DC on June 10, 1963 are a fitting tribute to what he sought to achieve for his country, as the 35th President of the United States:

"I speak of peace, therefore, as the necessary rational end of rational men... world peace, like community peace, does not require that each man love his neighbour – it requires only that they live together in mutual tolerance...our problems are man-made – therefore they can be solved by man. And man can be as big as he wants."

ABOVE: Lee Harvey Oswald outside his rented apartment with the gun he used to kill JFK and holding one of his 'protest' leaflets. (Warren Commission)

ABOVE: Jack Ruby ended all hope of getting the truth from Lee Harvey Oswald when he gunned him down in the basement of the Dallas Police Headquarters. (Author's collection)

CHAPTER TWELVE

BELOW: John F Kennedy's body is brought to the nation's capital for a lying in state. (NARA)

LEGACY

Kennedy entered office as the President of the United States with firm convictions that had been summed up in the New Frontiers programme, declared at his inaugural address on January 20, 1961 and in which social justice and welfare for deserving citizens was paramount. Within months he was embroiled in a space race, an arms race and crises in Berlin and later over Russian missiles in Cuba, while battling problems with Congress.

Standing for election on the left-leaning wing of the liberal Democratic Party, Kennedy carried the New Deal torch lit by his predecessor Franklin D Roosevelt. But instead of a clear run to those objectives, he found opposition in a coalition of Republicans and conservative southern Democrats in Congress who had had enough of old campaigns for radical change.

On the campaign trail, JFK proposed federal funds for elementary and secondary education for all, health insurance for the elderly, for the under privileged and for those dispossessed and rejected by a consumer-driven society. Over time, all those rights he fought so hard to bring about were championed by his successor, Lyndon Johnson, and his own drive, zealously prosecuted to establish the Great Society.

Yet many young people, inspired by Kennedy's appeal to "ask not what your country can do for you – ask what you can do for your country" joined the Peace Corps and went abroad on what today would be called gap-year assignments to help in Third World countries and as volunteers for medical aid organisations. Having seen the abject poverty of a post-war world torn by years of conflict and ideological revolution, many came back

ABOVE: The coat of the arms of the Kennedy family granted in 1961 by Gerald Slevin, Chief Herald of Ireland. (JFK Library)

104   JFK – A LIFE REMEMBERED

changed and some emigrated to the United States from those places, equally inspired by Kennedy's message.

The glamour and glitz of a privileged life sadly became the imprimatur of what was termed 'Camelot', the idealised Arthurian castle on a hill, but this one with John and Jackie in residence. It was no more representative of their real lives than was the legend of a mythical Camelot in classic literature. But the analogy did have a point. The sentimental ideal of 'knightly' service, duty to country and respect for human dignity idealised in the Old World European countries did seem to be at the core of the Kennedy message.

Over the next several decades, all those ideals would come to pass, if not on the scale and to the extent envisaged, nor with the general approval of all. But it can be truthfully said that both John and Robert Kennedy were significantly ahead of their time in espousing the virtues of an egalitarian and caring society. One built on

ABOVE: The Warren Commission completed its work on the assassination of JFK and submitted its findings on September 24, 1964 but many since have challenged its conclusions. (Warren Commission)

BELOW: The mark on the road in Dealey Plaza, Dallas, Texas, where President Kennedy was shot. (Adam Jones)

"The sentimental ideal of 'knightly' service, duty to country and respect for human dignity idealised in the Old World European countries did seem to be at the core of the Kennedy message."

the fruits of labour, commitment and to the old early 19th century American dream of a New Frontier.

TO SERVE…

Led by Sargent Shriver, husband of JFK's sister Eunice, the Peace Corps allowed American citizens to apply for two years of service in a developing country with applicants being assigned places and organisations according to assessed skill levels. Those with marketing skills went to teach new businesses, medical students to monitor and support health care services, and educators to schools and to provide English-language lessons. In achieving this there was positive feedback to countries and people traditionally suspicious of America's intentions, sowing goodwill, and a sense of inclusion for many who saw the United States as merely opportunistic. For some, it was a hard message to sell.

Long after his Presidency, what Kennedy began in the Peace Corps programme spilled laterally across to government agencies keen to work with foreign countries, each perhaps equally suspicious of the 'brain drain' or of US patent-theft, as joint ventures in science and engineering were sometimes referred to by cynics! In several countries where the Peace Corps worked, Kennedy's 10-year Alliance for Progress initiative helped engage trust with suspicious workers in places where it had been felt that the US government had supported despots and revolutionaries for America's economic, political, or military gain.

Roosevelt's Good Neighbor Policy of 1938 was a programme aimed at embracing countries in Latin and Central America suspicious of US intervention, with trade and cooperation opening markets and supporting the exchange of goods. It emphasised non-intervention in the political or social affairs of these countries and sought

CHAPTER TWELVE

to change the way these people saw the United States.

It had informed Roosevelt's drive to aid Britain during the early years of World War Two, citing the humanitarian logic of providing a hose to a neighbour whose house was on fire. It struck a chord with Congress and the Lease-Lend programme was born in March 1941 which, for all its critics and flaws provided a sound basis for US cooperation with the British struggling for survival. At least until a largely isolationist Congress was shocked into action by the Japanese attack on Pearl Harbor on December 7, 1941, plunging America full tilt into war.

Kennedy's Alliance for Progress lived on long after his assassination, but it was increasingly regarded at home and abroad as a political instrument to deter communism and to some extent that was true. Kennedy himself believed passionately in American 'idealism', that friendship between free and democratic countries could together build a defence against totalitarianism and autocratic rule where the citizen was subservient to heady and ideological dogma.

The Alliance programme eventually became an instrument for achieving political purposes and itself became a tool for coercion and a means of installing leaders acceptable to the US government. In time it would be used at great length in Vietnam. It was eventually worn down by a Congress reluctant to support what was interpreted as socialism. It was voted down because Latin American countries were unprepared to adopt numerous reforms implicit within the programme, despite $10bn having been spent. It was replaced with an existing body, the Organization of American States formed in 1948, reawakening the concept of a union of American republics mooted in 1826 by José de San Martin and Simón Bolivar.

President Johnson seized the opportunity to demonstrate his vigour in completing JFK's work and set about using his considerable experience and influence in Congress to pass the late President's Civil Rights Bill into law. It banned all forms of discrimination on race and gender, in employment and on civil rights. Continuing JFK's pioneering work, he also signed the omnibus Economic Opportunity Act of 1964 which attacked the roots of poverty and set up a Jobs Corps for vocational training across the country.

As a domestic equivalent of the Peace Corps, Johnson saw through the Volunteers in Service to America (VISTA) programme for teacher support in impoverished regions across the United States. He also continued JFK's work on environmental conservation through the Wilderness Protection Act which saved 3.68m hectares (9.1m acres) across the US. Johnson also saw through

BELOW: President Johnson carried forward Kennedy's New Frontier programme as his drive for a 'Great Society' which saw the signing of the War on Poverty bill in 1964. (NAA)

to completion acts for providing additional funds for schools, for setting up the Medicare programme to offset health costs for the elderly and the Omnibus Housing Act building homes for low income families.

In all, Johnson signed 84 separate bills, all of which had been part of the JFK-LBJ campaign message and on which Kennedy had been voted into office. When Johnson was elected on his own ticket in 1964, he received 61% of the popular vote, more than any other in history and 90.3% of the electoral vote. Essentially to the right of the Democratic Party, Johnson campaigned for low tax and small government. His ideals, however, were solidly aligned with those of JFK and he would have stood for a third term had he not been worn down and demoralised by the mire of the Vietnam war.

FOREIGN POLICY

Confrontation with the Soviet Union over the rights of Berlin and its division into US, British, French, and Russian sectors was considered to have come closer to war than the Cuban Missile Crisis, the latter more commonly remembered because of the worldwide publicity it received. Those two crises were integrated by Soviet belligerence over seemingly intractable issues created by the unpredictable Khrushchev. It fashioned the new White House leadership into a more robust and capable administration from which much else flowed.

Berlin had lasting repercussions and set the stage for the President's historic speech to its citizens on June 26, 1963 when he gave hope to an isolated people, revisited by President Ronald Reagan who, on June 12, 1987, made an appeal to the general secretary of the Soviet Communist Party: "Mr Gorbachev, tear down this wall!" In a little over two years it was gone, shortly followed by Gorbachev himself. Just as a failure to achieve what he sought had brought about the demise of Khrushchev two decades earlier. But there were other areas of test and challenge, as yet not as widely covered by the world's media but which would grow to outrank Berlin and Cuba.

One of the defining aspects of Kennedy's foreign policy decisions was the agony with which he debated the use of American troops in Southeast Asia, and Vietnam in particular. On several fronts, this one issue brought a tense disagreement with McNamara over the use of combat personnel and the way in which the US would manipulate governments and conduct regime change. While Kennedy was merely continuing policies and promises made by the Truman and Eisenhower administrations, McNamara brought a new and clinical assessment based on computerised evaluations and spreadsheet analysis rather than through precedent and the recommendations of advisers.

The lesson over Berlin and the stand he made on Cuba cemented a strong conviction in Kennedy's rationale regarding the acceptance of communist influence around the world. After World War Two, US foreign policy was heavily influenced by the need to contain communism by the so-called 'domino' theory in which if one country fell to communism another would follow and so on. In 1955 the South East Asia Treaty Organisation (SEATO) was formed to contain communist expansion.

Through this programme, President Eisenhower had sent 700 military personnel to South Vietnam to help it contain aggressive moves from the communist North Vietnam. It did not go well, and Kennedy inherited a mess. A catholic, South Vietnamese leader Ngo Dinh Diem and his repression of the Buddhists brought civil strife and Kennedy approved the transfer of 16,000 military advisers to help him shore up his regime. As the situation worsened, in September 1963 Kennedy offered his view about Vietnam, a prescient reflection on why American troops were there and why they would stay:

"In the final analysis, it is their war. They are the ones who have to win it or lose it. We can help them, we can give them equipment, we can send our men out there as advisers, but they have to win it, the people of Vietnam, against the communists...But I don't agree with those who say we should withdraw. That would be a great mistake... (The United States) made this effort to defend Europe. Now Europe is quite secure. We also have to participate – we may not like it – in the defence of Asia."

A coup orchestrated by agents of the US government and internal sympathisers to the American position overthrew the government of South Vietnam on November 1, 1963 and Diem was assassinated. Diem had been offered a way out if he resigned but he did not, and chaos prevailed for two years before Nguyen Van Thieu became Prime Minister in 1965.

We cannot be sure whether Kennedy would have withdrawn troops, increased

ABOVE: All his life, Johnson fought against poverty and under his term in office he toured poor districts and engaged with the underdog, bringing more bills helping the homeless and the destitute than any other President in history. (NARA)

ABOVE: Lyndon Johnson signing into law the Medicare Bill he fought to get through Congress. The bill perpetuated the legacy of both his and JFK's ambition for better health provision for the elderly and the poor. (NARA)

CHAPTER TWELVE

ABOVE: Throughout the 1960s, President Johnson was in a constant struggle between domestic issues in social care, increased pressure from foreign affairs and an escalating war in Southeast Asia, accompanied here by Dean Rusk (left) and Robert McNamara. (NARA)

ABOVE: Pierre Salinger (left) with Lyndon Johnson as they agree a press release with staffers and aides. (NARA)

communist guerrillas seeking to gain control of the country. Fellow communists in North Vietnam provided assistance.

President Eisenhower made great effort to support the Laotian government and managed to get a peace treaty concluded, with mixed results. Almost immediately civil war broke out and in 1962 the Kennedy administration presided over a negotiated settlement with Russia. Nevertheless, brushfire action continued unabated and the opening of the Ho Chi Minh trail from eastern Laos resulted in a conduit for arms to communist insurgents in South Vietnam.

Under Johnson, the bombing of Laos was justified on the basis of that arms conduit until a ceasefire agreement was signed in 1973. Two years later the Pathet Lao took control of Laos as the North Vietnamese unified Vietnam. Ironically, as preached by McNamara the domino effect had been real, but it worked in reverse by uniting communist elements of Southeast Asia into an integrated stand against Western powers, something they never envisaged would happen to them when the French were forced to flee in 1954.

As for Cuba, Castro never did accept the removal of Russia's ballistic missiles and became more vocal in condemnation of American policy, seeking to develop a country outside the shackles of superpower control. Many good things would come out of Cuba, the country becoming a world exemplar for botanical and agricultural research and the scientific study of organic nutrients and sustainable food production.

The Americans learned to live with their pro-communist neighbour and over time various US government administrations sought to improve relations. In the beginning, during the early months of the Kennedy administration there had been many voices urging an invasion and the restoration of American control. Several US business owners had made their fortunes over Cuba, not least Juan Trippe, founder

levels of military support or pulled back. High-placed officials who were part of this unfolding drama are divided as to what he would done. It could be said that he would perhaps have been more resolute and taken a hard line against the North Vietnamese and their allies, but we will never know. As it was, by 1968 the number of US forces in the war had grown to exceed 500,000 with 58,000 American dead before the retreat in 1975 and the surrender of the South to the North.

Somewhat peripheral to the story of Vietnam, Laos had become a problem early in Kennedy's Presidency. As with Vietnam, after World War Two the French had attempted to regain their old colonies and to reassert domination over Indochina which included Laos and Cambodia. When the French were thrown out of Vietnam and Laos in 1954, a Geneva accord gave Lao sovereignty but after a civil war the Royal Lao government fought off Pathet Lao

ABOVE: Led to an escalating conflict in Vietnam by Robert McNamara (right), Johnson wrestled with deep-seated challenges while his secretary of defence became increasingly disenchanted with the campaign and resigned on February 29, 1968. (NARA)

of Pan American World Airways who built his business on flying pleasure-seeking Americans from Key West, Florida, to Havana, Cuba.

From the 1920s, Cuba had been the playground for US mafia-gangs running brothels, casinos, drug-dealing syndicates and with freely available alcohol when prohibition was in force across most American states. Regularly scheduled flights transported wealthy Americans eager to engage in activities illegal in the United States. The Kennedy's balanced pressure from many groups wanting to restore access with calls from groups invoking moral outrage at how the island had been exploited under the Batista regime. One more set of challenges that spun a complex web of intrigue.

SPACE TO EXPLORE

As related in chapter five, Kennedy was reluctant to engage fully with the nascent space programme, a technical endeavour that had exploded on the world with the launch of Sputnik in October 1957. He was doubtful about the value of a follow-on programme to NASA's one-man Mercury spacecraft, as President Eisenhower had been. It is doubtful whether the initiation of the Apollo programme would have occurred had Russia not launched Yuri Gagarin into orbit less than three months before Kennedy's inauguration.

The decision not only to fund Apollo but also to assign it to a lunar landing before the end of that decade came in direct response to Gagarin's flight and to the embarrassment of the attempted invasion of Cuba at the Bay of Pigs, which proved disastrous. Some might say the Moon decision was a knee-jerk reaction while Kennedy was distracted by the Soviet achievements. Others would say that he had a prescient view of what was necessary to leapfrog the Russians.

But a few might say that it was a purely political move, a clinical decision to raise the standing of the United States following two embarrassing events, only one of which had anything to do with space. And they may well be correct. As the reality of the challenge became evident, Kennedy began to lose faith in what he had begun. Absent the inspired and seminal speeches he made on space activities, his 'new frontier' approach to space exploration was pragmatic, even-handed, and focused.

Kennedy saw the space programme largely as Congress did, a one-time event to beat the Russians at their own game. By starting in on the Moon landing, which in many ways was quite separate to existing space programmes already well underway, Kennedy deflected the nation's effort away from what had been referred to as the 'von Braun paradigm'.

Espoused by former German rocket engineer Wernher von Braun and architect of the Saturn rocket programme, orbital flights with crewed vehicles would precede Earth orbiting space stations followed by Moon reconnaissance flights and a landing on the surface. In deciding to leap from not having even achieved manned orbital flight direct to a Moon landing, Kennedy destabilised the logic of sequential technical progress and side-tracked the programme into what many regarded as a cul-de-sac. A place in which a lot that could have been achieved of a more permanent basis was left undeveloped or at best postponed.

NASA wanted Apollo to spark a permanent presence on the lunar surface. Congress wanted to achieve a political goal to raise a technological virility symbol to uncommitted nations. It did not want a 'permanent' anything and after that goal had been achieved it consistently voted down funds for continuing with manned exploration of the Moon. Many at NASA, and advocates of manned space flight today, felt that opportunity had been lost along with the massive investment in vehicles and infrastructure funded for Apollo by government taxes.

The legacy of Apollo lay in the surge of space technology around the world which was quickly put to good use for people on Earth, through improved weather forecasting, Earth resource studies, environmental monitoring, communications, and navigation systems. All those came along despite the Apollo programme but quicker because of it. And it stimulated new industries across the world as major powers followed America and developed their own space programmes providing basic applications.

As for the linear progression of manned flight, that saw development of the partially reusable Space Shuttle and 133 successful flights between 1981 and 2011, supporting orbital assembly of the International Space

ABOVE: Johnson visited troops at Cam Ranh Bay in Vietnam on October 26, 1966 and engaged with units to convey a message of support in a war already running out of options. (DoD)

ABOVE: Some decisions by Robert McNamara came good, as eventually did the General Dynamics F-111, seen here in operation with the US Air Force. (USAF)

CHAPTER TWELVE

ABOVE: The great challenge posed by JFK was realised at the end of the 1960s by the Apollo Moon landing programme, the expansive facilities at Cape Canaveral being named the John F Kennedy Space Center, affectionately referred to simply as KSC. (NASA)

Station which has been permanently manned since 2000. Perhaps the von Braun paradigm has finally been adopted, with NASA now developing the Artemis programme to set up sustainable bases on the Moon, returning but on a more permanent basis and this time with international partners.

But from the outset, not long after Kennedy declared the Moon as a 'frontier' goal in May 1961, there were misgivings regarding the cost of the Apollo programme and the way in which it appeared to Kennedy to be an excessive use of resources. By 1963 so much more was already being achieved by NASA, in development of communication satellites and planetary exploration that Kennedy began to question the necessity and the risk of pressing forward with the original goal.

As related earlier, Kennedy wanted to fully explore the possibility of merging US and Soviet space programmes and had moved discussion to a serious consideration of that just before he was assassinated. Under Johnson that idea was quickly buried, but the legacy was in the joint flight between US and Soviet spacecraft in 1975 as part of a new era of détente and an emerging policy of mutual coexistence.

THE ARMS RACE

Defined by Kennedy and put in place by his defence secretary Robert McNamara, the shift away from 'massive retaliation' to the strategic policy of 'flexible response' transformed the armed services. The legacy was set when McNamara carried through important decisions regarding the type of equipment to develop, and that played a central role in manoeuvring the US Air Force in particular to a new way of thinking about conventional and nuclear warfare.

Kennedy inherited a rapidly evolving equipment dilemma – how to integrate into a single strategic deterrent the new era of ballistic missiles on land and at sea with the more conventional bomber force which until the late 1950s had been the only means of long-range delivery for nuclear weapons. Eisenhower's policy of 'massive retaliation' was a legacy of World War Two, totally unsuited to the new age of rockets and missiles. The transition away from that enabled a broader political flexibility in response to national crises involving arms such as confrontations over Berlin and Cuba.

The legacy of that transition was to see the proliferation of smaller, tactical nuclear weapons on delivery systems capable of highly accurate targeting. Reluctant to fully roll back the expansion of strategic nuclear weapons, Kennedy set in motion an escalation which was itself much less than that sought by the Pentagon. However, in

ABOVE: President Johnson and Vice President Agnew were at the launch of Apollo 11 on July 16, 1969. It had been Johnson who managed the legislation establishing NASA in 1958 and he led the effort to get Kennedy to announce the Moon goal three years later. (NASA)

doing so he set in train a procurement and deployment plan which would retain US superiority for the next decade, the Russians only matching US arsenals by the mid-1970s.

In the overall rating of policy changes, Kennedy introduced new and effective means of additional layers of national security, adding specialised agencies to handle the new age of missiles, rockets, and satellites. One of which was the National Reconnaissance Office set up in September 1961 to control operational requirements and handling of intelligence from America's spy satellites. The NRO was a vital source of centralised information gathered without affiliation to any of the separate armed services.

Eisenhower had been concerned over the manipulation of data and statistics raised to support budget bids in Congressional hearings. There had been no coherent and agnostic interpretation of evidence and that resulted in the 'bomber gap' scare and the 'missile gap' myth, which had itself been used by Kennedy to criticise the Republican stance. But the needs of an electoral campaigner are different from those of a President, and he quickly changed his mind when attaining office. Ironically recognising his own misuse of data as a reason for setting up the NRO!

At an equipment level, McNamara made some grave mistakes that redirected development of aircraft types. In particular his attempt to save money by combining air force and navy requirements for a long range fighter – the infamous TFX programme that resulted in the swing-wing F-111. Designed to operate from both fixed land bases and aircraft carriers, it was impossibly compromised and resulted in cancellation of the navy version. That led to the F-14 Tomcat in service from late 1974, wasting many years and redefining future US Air Force and US Navy concepts thereafter.

In its own variant of F-111, the air force inherited a superb strike aircraft and for a while operated the FB-111 strategic bomber variant. Wisely but against opposition from the bomber-fraternity, McNamara did cancel the B-70, a high-flying Mach 3+ strategic bomber which quickly became redundant to purpose in the advancing age of air defence missiles capable of striking down any such intruder. Impossibly complex and in many respects ahead of extant technology, it would been a nightmare to integrate into the existing inventory.

Policy changes came thick and fast during the Kennedy administration. The war in Southeast Asia into which the armed services were tipped would see a seismic transformation in the way succeeding administrations would handle both equipment procurement and strategy. It would culminate in the doctrine of 'flexible response' cascading down into all aspects of defence and national security.

The Kennedy administration set the scene for a massive escalation in nuclear weapons but on a political level showed that it was possible to stare-down Soviet belligerence and find a way of working with an opponent. Directed by Kennedy, McNamara's lasting legacy was in the way nuclear war was placed further down the list of options available to the national command and those making seminal decisions about conflict. For that alone, the world can be eternally grateful.

BELOW: While expressing doubts about the Apollo Moon programme in the last year of his life, JFK failed to see the goal he challenged Americans to accept with the first landing on July 20, 1969, for many a fitting legacy to the life of John Fitzgerald Kennedy. (NASA)

CHAPTER THIRTEEN

THE TIMELINE OF A LIFE

The following chronology lists key events in the life and times of John Fitzgerald Kennedy and includes family births and deaths together with national and international events as they affected JFK's presidency. Some details are not covered in the preceding chapters. It is intended as a general reference source to be used while reading the narrative story.

SEPTEMBER 6, 1888
Joseph Patrick Kennedy Snr is born in East Boston, Massachusetts

JULY 22, 1890
Rose Fitzgerald is born in Boston, Massachusetts

OCTOBER 7, 1914
Joseph Kennedy marries Rose Fitzgerald

JULY 25, 1915
Joseph Patrick 'Joe' Kennedy is born, no children, dies August 12, 1944

MAY 29, 1917
JFK is born in Brookline, Massachusetts, four children, assassinated November 22, 1963

JUNE 19, 1917
JFK is baptised at St Aidan's Church

SEPTEMBER 13, 1918
Rose Marie 'Rosemary' Kennedy is born, no children, died January 7, 2005

FEBRUARY 20, 1920
Kathleen Agnes 'Kick' Kennedy is born, no children, died May 13, 1948

JULY 10, 1921
Eunice Mary Kennedy is born, five children, died August 11, 2009

MAY 6, 1924
Patricia Helen 'Pat' Kennedy is born, four children, died September 17, 2006

NOVEMBER 20, 1925
Robert F 'Bobby' Kennedy is born, 11 children, assassinated June 6, 1968

SEPTEMBER, 1927
Kennedy family moves to Riverdale, NY

OCTOBER, 1929
Great Depression hits families and businesses.

SEPTEMBER, 1931
JFK enrols in Choate School, Wallingford, Connecticut

FEBRUARY 22, 1932
Edward Moore 'Ted' Kennedy is born, three children, died August 25, 2009

JUNE, 1934
JFK admitted to Mayo Clinic with colitis

JUNE, 1935
JFK graduates from Choate, ranked 64th in a class of 112

SEPTEMBER, 1935
JFK travels to London with his parents and Kathleen

SEPTEMBER, 1936
JFK enrols at Harvard Collage

1937
Joseph Kennedy Snr is named ambassador to Great Britain

FEBRUARY 23, 1938
Joseph Kennedy Snr sails for England, waved off by JFK

JULY, 1938
JFK and his brother Joseph Kennedy II sailed to England, tours Europe

SEPTEMBER 1, 1939
Germany invades Poland

SEPTEMBER 3, 1939
Britain declares war on Germany

1940
JFK writes his senior thesis, on English foreign policy prior to World War Two

JULY 24, 1940
JFK's thesis is published, under the title *Why England Slept*

SEPTEMBER 24, 1941
JFK joins the US Naval Reserve

OCTOBER 25, 1941
JFK commissioned an ensign and joins Office of Naval Intelligence

DECEMBER 7, 1941
Japanese bomb Pearl Harbor, US declares war on Germany and Japan

DECEMBER 7, 1942
JFK gets command of PT-101

APRIL 24, 1943
JFK takes command of PT-109

AUGUST 2, 1943
JFK's PT boat is rammed by a Japanese destroyer. Under his leadership, most of the crew is eventually rescued. JFK receives the Purple Heart for his heroics

1944
JFK enters Boston's Chelsea Naval Hospital with a lower back condition

AUGUST 12, 1944
Joseph Kennedy, Jnr is killed while flying a mission over Europe

MARCH 1, 1945
JFK is discharged from the Navy

CHRONOLOGY

(AARON SHICKLER)

JUNE 17, 1946
JFK wins the Democratic primary for Massachusetts' Eleventh Congressional District

NOVEMBER 5, 1946
JFK is elected to the House of Representatives

NOVEMBER 2, 1948
JFK is elected to a second term in the House. While on a trip to England, he is diagnosed with Addison's Disease. His condition is kept secret from the public

JUNE 25, 1950
Korean War breaks out when the North invades the South

FEBRUARY 1950
Wisconsin Senator Joseph McCarthy claims to have a list of communists employed in the State Department. The era of 'McCarthyism' begins

NOVEMBER 1950
JFK is elected to a third term in the House

NOVEMBER 4, 1952
JFK defeats Henry Cabot Lodge, Jnr to win election to the United States Senate. In the presidential election, Dwight Eisenhower and his running mate, Richard Nixon, defeat Adlai Stevenson

SEPTEMBER 12, 1953
JFK marries Jacqueline Bouvier

DECEMBER 2, 1954
Joseph McCarthy is censured by the US Senate. JFK abstains from voting on the resolution

1955-1956
JFK 'writes' *Profiles in Courage*, a history of heroic American senators. In fact, the book is largely written by his speechwriter, Theodore Sorensen

SUMMER 1956
At the Democratic National Convention, Tennessee Senator Estes Kefauver edges JFK out to become Adlai Stevenson's running mate

AUGUST 23, 1956
Arabella Kennedy is the stillborn daughter of Jack and Jackie Kennedy

NOVEMBER 1956
Eisenhower crushes Stevenson and wins re-election

1957
Profiles in Courage is awarded the Pulitzer Prize

NOVEMBER 27, 1957
Caroline Bouvier Kennedy, JFK's daughter, is born

NOVEMBER 4, 1958
JFK wins re-election to the Senate by a comfortable margin

JULY 1960
JFK wins the Democratic nomination for president and picks Lyndon Johnson as his running mate

NOVEMBER 8, 1960
JFK defeats Nixon and becomes President

NOVEMBER 25, 1960
Birth of John F. Kennedy, Jnr. Dies July 16, 1999

JANUARY 20, 1961
John F. Kennedy is sworn in as the 35th President of the United States

JANUARY 21, 1961
JFK meets with former President Harry S Truman and signs an order doubling the surplus food given to needy families

JANUARY 25, 1961
JFK holds the first in a regular series of live TV press conferences

JANUARY 30, 1961
JFK delivers his first 'State of the Union' address to a Joint Session of Congress

MARCH 1, 1961
JFK announces the establishment of the Peace Corps

APRIL 12, 1961
Russia launches first human into space

APRIL 17, 1961
Attempted US-backed invasion of Cuba ends in disaster at the Bay of Pigs

(NARA)

CHAPTER THIRTEEN

MAY 5, 1961
Astronaut Alan Shepard makes the first US space flight, a ballistic flight lasting 15 minutes, clearing a way for the Moon decision

MAY 8, 1961
JFK awards astronaut Shepard with the NASA Distinguished Service Medal

MAY 25, 1961
JFK announces Apollo Moon goal to a Joint Session of Congress

JUNE 3-4, 1961
JFK and Russian Premier Nikita Khrushchev hold a summit in Vienna

JUNE 4-5, 1961
JFK visits Britain and meets Queen Elizabeth II

JULY 25, 1961
In a television address, JFK says he is not seeking conflict over Berlin

AUGUST 13, 1961
East German and Russian troops close the border with West Berlin

AUGUST 1961
USA and Latin American nations join in the 'Alliance for Progress'

SEPTEMBER 25, 1961
In an address to the United Nations, JFK claims he is challenging "the Soviet Union not to an arms race, but to a peace race."

OCTOBER 27, 1961
NASA launches the first Saturn I 'super-booster' which begins to put America toward leadership in space

FEBRUARY 20, 1962
John Glenn in a Mercury spacecraft becomes the first American to orbit the Earth

MARCH 1962
JFK forces the American steel industry to rescind a price increase

MAY 19, 1962
Marilyn Monroe sings "Happy Birthday Mr President", 10 days before the event

OCTOBER 16, 1962
The US obtains photographs of Soviet missile emplacements in Cuba, bringing about the Cuban Missile Crisis

OCTOBER 22, 1962
JFK announces naval quarantine of Cuba

OCTOBER 28, 1962
Soviet Union agrees to remove its missiles from Cuba

JUNE 1963
JFK calls civil rights struggle a "moral crisis" for America

JUNE 26, 1963
JFK makes a speech at the Berlin wall saying in German: "I am a Berliner."

AUGUST 5, 1963
US and the Soviet Union agree to a nuclear test-ban treaty

AUGUST 7, 1963
Patrick Bouvier Kennedy born, dies two days later.

OCTOBER 7, 1963
JFK signs the Partial Test Ban Treaty with the Soviet Union prohibiting all nuclear tests other than underground detonations

NOVEMBER 2, 1963
US-backed coup overthrows the government of South Vietnam, replaces it with a military dictatorship

NOVEMBER 11, 1963
JFK makes his final visit to Cape Canaveral and sees the Saturn rocket SA-5 which in 1964 will provide lift capability equalling that of the Soviet Union's rockets

NOVEMBER 22, 1963
JFK is assassinated while riding through the streets of Dallas, Texas. Lyndon Johnson becomes the 36th President of the United States

NOVEMBER 25, 1963
JFK is laid to rest at Arlington National Cemetery

(CAROL HIGHSMITH)